OpenBSD Mastery: Filesystems

Michael W Lucas

Tilted
Windmill
Press

Copyright Information

OpenBSD Mastery: Filesystems

Brief Contents

Complete Contents

Acknowledgements

This book would not exist if other people hadn't provided information up front. Claudio Jeker gave me the inside scoop on OpenBSD's iscsi stack. Stefan Sperling, Otto Moerbeek, and Ken Westerback offered insight and illumination on how OpenBSD manages disks. The hitchhikers of bsd.network offered a constant stream of details and experiences. Technical reviewers Tim Chase, Gabriel Guzman, Peter Hansteen, Lennart Jablonka, Reinis Martinsons, and Neil Roza caught many of my mistakes. As always, Bob Beck provided a reliable source of heckling disguised as color commentary.

A bunch of folks wanted this book to exist so much that they paid extra before the book even existed. You'll find a complete list of my sponsors at the end of the book.

A handful of folks not only wanted this particular book to exist, they send me cash every month no matter *what* I'm working on. My inestimable Patronizers make my books happen. Kate Ebneter, Stefan Johnson, Jeff Marraccini, Eirik Øverby, and Phil Vuchetich supported this book so highly that I must blame them in both the electronic and print editions.

May every one of you always remember where you left your towel.

While my wife Liz needs no filesystem management skills—and, indeed, such skills would impair her happiness and well-being—this book is for her.

"In the beginning, Berkeley released Unix.
This has made a lot of vendors very angry,
and been widely regarded as a bad move."

—*The Hitchhikers' Guide to OpenBSD*

Chapter 0: Introduction

Filesystems are not the most important topic in system administration—but if you configure your persistent data storage badly, doing everything else correctly won't matter. A well–planned arrangement of disks invisibly simplifies a system administrator's life. Ill–configured filesystems remain an annoyance until the system is wiped and rebuilt. OpenBSD is no exception. Understanding how your disks work, and how to configure them to suit the system's workload, will make your life easier.

OpenBSD includes many standard tools for disk management. Its Unix File System has been continuously used for decades and is both robust and well–understood. While it lacks features found in newer filesystems like ZFS and btrfs, the OpenBSD developers have never been seriously interested in file system features. A file system should put data on disk. That data should be safely stored and reliably read. That's it. Error checking? Deduplication? No. The operating system has other tools for ensuring data integrity and compactness. *OpenBSD Mastery: Filesystems* will take you through best practices for managing disks on OpenBSD. You will learn not just which commands to run, but the context for making sound decisions on disk management.

Sysadmin Prerequisites

This book is written for system administrators interested in OpenBSD. I assume that you understand how to use your shell and basic Unix commands. No previous OpenBSD experience is required—in fact, experimenting with filesystems is a great way to get that initial OpenBSD experience.

You must learn about your chosen disk technologies on your own. OpenBSD runs on many types of hardware from the last twenty years. I can't possibly give a reasonable overview of the difference between them all and if I did, it would be obsolete before this book could reach you. I will discuss traditional "spinning rust" hard drives, SSD's, and NVMe, but the specifics of each change continuously.

The best way to learn is with a test machine. A virtual machine will get you started, but if you find yourself responsible for a system with a complicated storage arrangement, you really need a test system that resembles what you're managing in production. Test your understanding where it doesn't matter, so that when you make mistakes you don't cause downtime people will notice.

Any time you tamper with partitioning and filesystems, you run the risk of demolishing data. When you work on production systems, verify your off-system backups before touching anything related to storage. If I included the phrase "be prepared to restore from backup" everywhere it needs to be, this book would require several inconveniently large buildings to carry it around in.

Filesystems are intimately entwined with the underlying hardware. Today's hard drives still provide interfaces that resemble the punch cards used to drive looms in the 17th century, and occasionally software uses them. Managing filesystems requires you to understand where disks came from, and where they are now.

14

Legacy Disks

Primordial filesystems, including early versions of UFS, were designed with the assumption that the file system would be placed on a pack of rotating physical disks. The designs took advantage of a spinning disk's natural characteristics such as rotational speed and the number of disks in the pack. The inside of the disk responded faster than the outside, so critical files were placed there. Could the file system idle a disk? That depended on the disk's spin–up time. Disks were huge, heavy, and expensive. Every millimeter of spinning rust had to be carefully accounted for.

Early disks were defined by a *geometry*. Sysadmins used the disk's geometry to optimally configure the file system. The axle in the middle is a *spindle*. Very thin *platters* were stacked on the spindle. Each platter had its own head that read and wrote that platter's data. A *disk drive* or *disk pack* was a spindle with a stack of platters and heads. Each platter contained concentric rings of magnetic material, called *tracks*. All of the platters inside a hard drive were identical, so the tracks lined up above one another. A stack of tracks was called a *cylinder*. Each cylinder was divided into logical units called *sectors* or *blocks*. Multiple layers of the storage stack use the word "block" differently, so I'll use "sector." Each sector had a number, with sector zero at the beginning. Sector zero was reserved for the partition table. When the operating system accessed the drive, it first asked for sector zero so it knew how to use the storage. The combination of sectors, tracks, heads, and cylinders defined the disk geometry.

An engineer designing a system, whether a hard drive or a car or a building or anything, must set limits. A two-lane bridge can only support a certain number of tons. The engineer has no way of knowing that three decades later trucks will weigh twice as much or that the road will be eight lanes wide. Similarly a computing platform can only support components up to a certain size. We joke about the 640 KB memory limit in the original IBM PC, but it made sense at the time. Designing a computer to handle a gigabyte of RAM in the

1970s would have been delusional. The i386 platform's 4GB memory limit worked for decades, but eventually doomed the platform. Disks hit critical design limits at 504 MB, 8 GB, 2 TB, and more. Each time hardware hit a limit, engineers figured out how to weasel their way around it. Those workarounds must be coordinated between the hardware and the operating system.

Sometimes, the two parties do not want to cooperate.

For years, hard drive manufacturers and popular operating system developers agreed that no hard drive could have more than sixty-three sectors in a track. A clever manufacturer figured out how to cram 126 sectors into a track, doubling the capacity of their drives. Operating systems would not recognize the disk, however. If you're a manufacturer and you want to sell your great big hard drives to the users of popular operating systems, what do you do?

You teach your hard drive to lie.

Make the hard drive claim that it has only 63 sectors per track, but it has twice as many platters, or twice as many tracks. Either works, so long as the numbers add up. When your hard drive bumps up against another operating system limit, add another layer of lies. The lies are all maintained in code, so there is absolutely no way that any of them could cause trouble. Code always knows what it's doing.[1]

Once you accumulate enough layers of lies, and everyone expects you to lie, coming clean is hard.

Every hard drive manufacturer has chosen their preferred lies. Immobile solid-state disks claim to have cylinders, sectors, and tracks. Hardware RAID and virtual disk images create meticulously crafted lies to grant the operating system superpowers. Tracking all these lies fills thousands of lines of firmware source code.

Disk drives still come labeled with a geometry, but for decades that geometry has borne no resemblance to what is inside the drive. Filesystems like UFS still include references to that geometry, however.

---

[1]   If you believe this, please hand this book to someone who knows what they are doing.

The file system has no way of knowing what kind of lies a disk tells. For all it knows, the disk might even be telling the truth—but it's not. Ever.[2]

The Internet still has reams of advice on how to partition your disks to optimize performance according to the drive's geometry. This advice is all useless for any standard storage device built within the last twenty years. If you're running OpenBSD on some lovely retro computing hardware, including the original hard drives, seek out those tutorials. You can find my older technical books with that information very inexpensively at any used book dealer or landfill.

While geometry lingers, we have a better way.

Logical Block Addressing

Lies are unsustainable, so all modern hard drives use Logical Block Addressing (LBA). With LBA, every sector is assigned a number starting with zero. LBA lets you stop worrying about cylinders, heads, platters, and everything else that doesn't exist in your storage device. Instead, you identify sectors by number. The computer considers sectors as elements in an array, with zero regard for the physical layout.

LBA drives still report a traditional geometry, but everybody knows it is fictional. Many filesystems still make decisions based on geometry, however, so we're stuck with it.

Sector Size

Each sector on a disk has a size, dictating how much data can be stored in that sector. Through the 1990s, sector size ranged between 128 bytes to 2 kB. In the early 2000's, manufacturers converged on 512–byte sectors. Drives can now contain far larger amounts of data, so over the last ten years sector size has mostly increased to 4 KB.

The problem is that popular commercial operating systems knew that sectors were 512 bytes. If a hard drive reported it had 4 KB sectors, the operating system had a fit. Manufacturers coped with this the same way as always.

[2]   Rule of System Administration #13: All storage devices lie.

The new lies were bad enough, but different manufacturers told their drives to lie in different ways. Many drives claim they have 512–byte sectors. Some claim to have both 512–byte and 4 KB sectors. A handful of honest drives admit that they have 4 KB sectors. Many modern solid-state drives and NVMEs have sectors as large as 8 KB or 16 KB, or offer varying sector sizes for your inconvenience.

What does the sysadmin do about all this?

The same thing we always do. Cope.

Where some operating systems implement schemes to determine and respect a disk's actual sector size, OpenBSD pretty much assumes that all disks are liars and partitions everything as if the disk uses 4 KB sectors. This assumption wastes a few kilobytes of disk space here and there, but is negligible on modern disks. It also preserves the alignment between filesystem sectors and disk sectors. We will see the effect of this as we explore the different types of partitioning.

Disk Size

Not all one terabyte drives are the same size. The computing industry can't agree on how large a terabyte is, and the manufacturers have wholly different motivations then either operating system designers or sysadmins alike.

Computers are binary. Drive size should be computed in base two. This would make a one terabyte drive 1,024 gigabytes and each gigabyte 1,024 megabytes. Hard drive manufacturers measure storage size in base ten rather than base two, however, letting them claim their drives are larger than they are. Definitions like "tebibyte," while useful, have not caught on—in part, because drive manufacturers don't want them to.

Additionally, drives are not precisely the advertised size. If a drive is labeled as being one terabyte, meaning a base-ten terabyte, it's actually that base-ten terabyte plus a few extra sectors. Nobody complains about extra sectors, but customers already disgruntled by base ten terabytes would be infuriated if the drive was even smaller than that. So long as the total number of sectors rounds off to about the right size, the manufacturer is content. Two hard drives might both claim to be one terabyte, but one is probably a few sectors larger than the other. Users don't care until we need to replicate one drive on another. You cannot copy a hard drive's partition table onto a smaller hard drive.

If you are using large numbers of disks in a system, I recommend leaving a little bit of empty space at the end of the drive. This leaves you some slop space to accommodate slightly different drive sizes if you must duplicate the drive. We'll see this in Chapter 7.

TRIM

SSDs expect to know which sectors are no longer in use, so that they can perform efficient garbage collection. The TRIM command lets an operating system pass this information to the drive.

OpenBSD does not support TRIM, for a few reasons. Early TRIM implementations had an unacceptable performance impact on the operating system. Early drive firmware handled TRIM poorly, sometimes corrupting previously stored data. Finally, a clever intruder could abuse TRIM to gather information about disk encryption.

Time has shown that, in general, the TRIM approach is less desirable than originally hoped. Modern SSD drives have their own built-in garbage collectors, however, rendering TRIM unnecessary.

What's In This Book?

This introduction covered some basics about storage device terminology and the realities of modern disk design.

Chapter 1, *The OpenBSD Storage Stack*, discusses OpenBSD's storage stack. We will cover MBR and GPT partitioning schemes as used on amd64, i386, and several other architectures. We will discuss the basics of the BSD–specific disklabel partition used on all architectures and the device nodes used to identify them. The rest of this book, and all OpenBSD system administration, builds on this essential knowledge.

Chapter 2, *The Unix Filesystem*, gives an in-depth discussion of the standard OpenBSD filesystem UFS. You'll learn about the parts of UFS, the kinds of mounts, mounting, and adding disks.

Chapter 3, *Memory, Swap, and the Buffer Cache* covers how RAM is intimately entangled with filesystems, and how to manage their interactions. We'll cover memory filesystems, adding and removing swap, and why the buffer cache gives people headaches.

Chapter 4, *Foreign Filesystems*, discusses using filesystems not intended for OpenBSD. At some point you'll need to mount ISOs, or flash drives, or even modern Windows disks. OpenBSD has integrated support for many of these, and supports more through FUSE.

Chapter 5, *The Network File System*, introduces mounting filesystems from other hosts. NFS is a venerable Unix standard, and OpenBSD supports it solidly.

Chapter 6, *iSCSI*, will help when you need to mount an entire disk remotely.

Chapter 7, *Redundancy*, discusses configuring and managing software RAID with OpenBSD's softraid(4) interface and bioctl(8).

Finally, Chapter 8, *Encrypted Storage*, discusses encrypting partitions and full disks. Which is a misnomer, because full disk encryption doesn't cover whole disks.

Learn all this, and you'll be able to competently exercise OpenBSD's storage features. That will leave you plentiful free time to figure out actual applications. Onward!

"I came to OpenBSD for a week,
and got stuck for twenty-eight years."

—*The Hitchhiker's Guide to OpenBSD*

Chapter 1: The OpenBSD Storage Stack

While many Unix-like operating systems dump everything onto the disk and hope things work out, OpenBSD uses a meticulous partitioning scheme to improve confidentiality, integrity, and availability. Additionally, OpenBSD's multi–architecture design demands abstraction layers between the storage hardware and the user–visible file system. Taking a little time to understand these two systems and how they interact will greatly simplify your work as a system administrator.

Filesystems and disks are complicated in that before you understand how any one piece works, you must understand every other component of the system. We will walk through each piece slowly, but you can't skip around this chapter hoping to learn the topic. Everything is built on everything else. Relax and follow along.

Storage Layers

Like all operating systems, OpenBSD uses abstraction layers to separate the user–visible file system from the underlying hardware. OpenBSD keeps its storage stack as simple as possible. You do not get the fancy storage transformations available in the Logical Volume Managers used by other operating systems, but you are protected from the accompanying headaches.

The bottom layer of any storage stack is the physical hardware. Yes, all modern hard drives run their own operating system, but they are invisible to OpenBSD.[3] Each device is assigned a number, starting at zero.

---

[3]   Fortunately, we are not expected to reflash hard drives. Yet.

Your hardware architecture expects a certain partitioning method, which I'll call a *hardware partition*. Hardware partitions are defined for the convenience of the hardware. Systems descended from the primordial IBM PC rely on either the Master Boot Record (MBR) or GUID Partition Tables (GPT). Newer platforms like arm64 have also adopted GPT. If you are running OpenBSD on less common hardware, check that platform's manuals and the OpenBSD documentation to learn about its hardware–level partitioning. Don't try to use partitioning methods the hardware doesn't support.

While the previous two layers are all hardware–specific, we now have the first OpenBSD-specific layer: the *disklabel*. A disklabel is placed on a hardware partition, and subdivides the disk into OpenBSD partitions. Yes, the word *partition* refers to a subdivision in multiple layers of the disk. Be clear which layer you are working at.

An OpenBSD disklabel describes the whole disk, not a hardware partition. A disklabel can include references to physical partitions other than that reserved for OpenBSD. A GPT boot disk includes a FAT partition for the boot loader. In a standard install, the disklabel includes an entry for that partition. The hardware uses the native partitions to find the operating system, while OpenBSD uses the disklabel to manage storage.

OpenBSD represents both hardware and disklabel partitions by a *device node*. A device node lets the sysadmin declare "I am running this command on this exact partition." You can mount disks by using their device node.

Decades ago, disk numbering remained constant. If the disk the operating system saw as *sd0* contained the root file system, you could be confident that that drive would be *sd0* every time you booted the system. Removable media, like floppy and optical drives, were numbered separately from hard disks. This is no longer the case. Drive numbering can shuffle around a system, especially when you consider hot–pluggable storage like USB flash drives. Every disklabel includes a Disklabel Unique Identifier (DUID), a unique hexadecimal number that OpenBSD uses to identify a partition. Configuration files reference the DUID rather than a device node.

The problem with DUIDs is that they're unpronounceable and unmemorable. The most common name you'll see for partitions is the device node. We will start by discussing device nodes so that we have a common language, and then move our way up through the storage stack.

Device Nodes

A *device node* is a file that provides a logical interface to a piece of hardware. Reading from a device node extracts data from the hardware. Writing to the device node sends data to the hardware. What happens to the data depends on the hardware. Not all device nodes do both: it makes no sense to read data from a speaker, for example. Disks are pretty straightforward—you read and write to them. OpenBSD puts device nodes in `/dev` and forbids them everywhere else.[4]

Device nodes are a common feature across Unixes. Many programs expect to be given a device node as an argument. Unfortunately, device node names range from cryptic to occult. For every meaningful `/dev/speaker` we have dozens of entries like `/dev/rvnd3q`. The device node names used on one Unix variant often bear no resemblance to those used on another Unix, and similar-looking ones might refer to entirely different hardware. Don't let muscle memory from another Unix betray you on OpenBSD.

Each device node starts with a name giving the type of hardware the node represents, often followed by a number indicating which piece of equipment this is. `/dev/speaker` represents the computer's speakers. Most computers have only one set of speakers at a time. The `/dev/sd` devices represent modern hard drives, and so are followed by a number. `/dev/sd0` is the first hard drive the system found at boot, `/dev/sd1` is the second, and so on.

The top of the script `/dev/MAKEDEV` lists all device nodes.

---

4   Certain mount flags can change "forbidden" to "foolish."

Common Device Names

While the sd device is the most common today, you will also encounter a few others. Here are the device node names for OpenBSD disk–type devices as of OpenBSD 7.2.

cd   optical drives
fd   floppy disks
rd   memory disks
wd   IDE disks, and SATA disks that pretend to be IDE
sd   SCSI, SAS, SATA, RAID, NVMe, and other non—IDE disks
vnd filesystem images

Each type of device node has a man page. If you want to know about `/dev/vnd` devices, run `man vnd`.

You will also see letters after drive device nodes. These represent partitions, as we will see later this chapter.

Raw and Block Devices

Disks expect the operating system device driver to request data by entire sectors. If the operating system wants to read the disk's MBR partition table, it commands the disk to send the contents of LBA sector zero. The hardware is optimized to process requests on a sector–by–sector basis. The standard device node is called a *block device*, or occasionally a *cooked device*.[5]

Sometimes, you don't want to be efficient. Sometimes, a program needs to dump data to the disk using a very specific buffering or in a particular pattern. You are accessing the disk as a *raw device*. This is increasingly rare, but occasionally you will encounter a program that expects to use the raw device. Raw devices have the same device name as the block device, with an *r* in front of the name. Device `sd0` is a block device. Device `rsd0` represents the exact same hardware, accessed in raw mode. Partition `/dev/sd0a` represents the exact same

---

[5]   Yes, yet another meaning of the word "block."

I would suggest giving every developer a thesaurus and making them use it, but that would merely give us a differently dreadful end.

partition as /dev/rsd0a. Choose the mode you access the device in by picking the device node.

Use the raw device node *only* if a program demands it. Almost all modern software is written for block devices. OpenBSD's device nodes are generated at install and/or upgrade, and OpenBSD provides the raw devices just in case they are needed. Their presence does not mean they should be used.

Insufficient Device Nodes

OpenBSD does not dynamically create device nodes. It has a set of defaults that are good enough for most users, but if you need additional device nodes you must create them. It ships with device nodes sd0 through sd9, supporting ten disks, and does not dynamically create new device nodes. If you have more than ten disks, you'll run out of device nodes. In Chapter 7 I'll boot from the install disk and have the same problem for disk sd0.

```
# fdisk sd10
fdisk: opendev('sd10', 0x0): No such file or directory
```

There is no device node /dev/sd10. Create more device nodes as needed with the /dev/MAKEDEV script. Give the device node as an argument. It will create all necessary files for the device, including partitions and raw nodes.

```
# cd /dev
# sh MAKEDEV sd10
```

You must create each node individually. Running sh MAKEDEV sd20 won't create device nodes sd10 through sd19, you must run the command eleven times.

Physical Disks

If installed disks can change at any time, how do you see which disks are currently on the system? Many people reach for dmesg.boot, but that is a static file and only represents what was installed at boot time. The dmesg(8) command displays the kernel messages currently in buffer, but you might have inserted and removed multiple storage devices in the buffer's lifetime. For accurate information on currently installed disks, check the sysctl `hw.disknames`.

```
$ sysctl hw.disknames
hw.disknames=sd0:d25c4224901b9485,sd1:,sd2:
```

This host has three disks. Disk *sd0* has a DUID, so it is an OpenBSD disk. Disks *sd1* and *sd2* have no DUID, so they are not OpenBSD disks. They might have partitions for other operating systems, or they might be blank.

To see how many disks are available, check the sysctl `hw.diskcount`.

Physical Disk Partitioning Schemes

Most operating systems and hardware platforms can subdivide hard drives into partitions. These hardware–level partitions are especially useful for people who want to run multiple operating systems on a single computer. If you look at a consumer laptop with a Microsoft operating system, you will probably see that the hard drive has been divided into partitions for reinstalling from scratch, hibernation, the user–visible operating system, and perhaps even a little something special from the vendor that need not concern you. Partitioning a disk might seem trivial, but even a sysadmin with a brain the size of a planet knows that correctly dividing the disk increases system longevity.

A partitioning scheme is a system for organizing partitions on the disk. Each scheme defines its own methods for boot blocks, partitions, redundancy, and more. The venerable MBR is perhaps the best–known partitioning scheme, even though it is not suitable for disks over 2TB. GPT is another. Apple and SPARC hardware use other schemes.

OpenBSD uses physical partitions as little as possible. A default OpenBSD install has nine partitions, and not all hardware partitioning schemes support that many partitions. Most disks, of any hardware architecture, are formatted with a single hardware–specific partition that covers the entire disk. Disklabel partitions are free of architecture–specific partitioning restrictions and are thus more suitable for OpenBSD.

OpenBSD uses fdisk to manage both MBR and GPT partitions. We will discuss each separately.

MBR Partitions

The Master Boot Record, or MBR, monopolizes the first 512 bytes or sector zero of a traditional disk. MBR was the standard for the original IBM PC. The MBR contains hardware–level partitioning information about the drive, as well as a very simple boot loader that allows the system BIOS to find the operating system. The term MBR can refer to either sector zero on the drive or the partitioning format.

An MBR partition table can support up to four primary partitions, and more through dividing one of them up into extended partitions. The partition table includes the disk sectors included in the partition and the file system on the partition. OpenBSD filesystems have a dedicated identifier for MBR partition tables.

The MBR format only supports drives up to two terabytes. Typical solid-state drives will soon exceed that, and finding spinning rust that small is becoming a challenge. Tiny systems might use MBR, but the scheme is ultimately doomed.

An MBR–partitioned disk can have up to one active partition. When the hardware powers on, the disk's boot loader code looks for the active partition and tries to boot it. An MBR disk without an active partition is not a boot drive.

OpenBSD normally partitions drives with a single active partition that covers the entire drive, leaving the other three partitions empty. The only reason to have multiple MBR partitions is if you are booting multiple operating systems on this hardware, which is very rare now that virtualization software is so common.

Only use MBR partitions if your system does not support GPT.[6]

---

[6]   As GPT has been around since the late 1990s, if you have an MBR–only system might I suggest returning to that dumpster and looking for something slightly newer?

GPT Partitions

GUID Partition Tables, or GPT, is the modern standard for disk partitioning. GPT supports disks up to 9.4 zettabytes. One zettabyte is 1 billion terabytes. Drives will eventually outgrow this limit, but my career will end before this so it is officially Somebody Else's Problem. Use GPT partitions unless doing so is impossible.

A GPT can have any number of partitions. Each partition is assigned a globally unique identifier, or GUID. A GUID is a 128-bit number, displayed as thirty-two hexadecimal digits, that is unique to this specific partition.

Hardware that understands MBR expects to find a Master Boot Record in the first sector of every disk. If the first sector of the disk doesn't have an MBR, the computer will get very depressed and complain endlessly. A GPT–partitioned disk puts a fake MBR in sector zero. This *protective MBR*, or PMBR, declares that the disk contains one MBR partition, of type GPT. OpenBSD uses a standard, blank MBR, including boot code, as the PMBR. The second sector, sector one, contains the actual GUID Partition Table.

The GPT designers learned from MBR's mistakes. Every disk that uses GPT keeps a backup copy of the partition table at the very end of the disk. If you damage the front of your disk, partitioning software can read the secondary GPT and recover the partition table. It might not save your data, especially as OpenBSD uses a single GPT partition per disk, but a little bit of hope is always nice.

If a GPT disk is intended as a boot drive, the first partition on the disk will be a tiny *Extensible Firmware Interface* (EFI) system partition. This contains the boot loader that finds the real operating system. The EFI partition uses a FAT–based file system. Mounting the EFI partition and mucking around with it is a great way to render your system non-bootable, but it's also a fabulous learning experience.

The world performed a slow migration from MBR to GPT. While everything you'll buy these days supports GPT, the migration path various operating systems used affects us today. Some operating systems supported booting GPT disks from MBR-only hosts. OpenBSD is not one of those. If you find you can't boot a GPT disk, verify that your host has "EFI" or "UEFI" enabled. Real hardware does this by default, but some virtualization software doesn't.

Avoiding Hardware Partitions

You might have heard ancient tales on exotic forums of installs that skipped hardware partitioning and wrote an OpenBSD disklabel straight on the disk. It's most often called "dangerously dedicated" mode. Some people want to try this, for reasons that are unlikely to become clear.

You hear about it only on sketchy forums is because it is not part of OpenBSD. "Dangerously dedicated" mode was a FreeBSD feature, not OpenBSD. It's been unnecessary for decades, but no less dangerous. Neither the software nor the hardware expects to use, let alone boot from, disks without hardware partitions. While it's poor practice to surprise your hardware or operating system, ambushing both simultaneously encourages them to team up against you. While a clever sysadmin could certainly wrangle a label directly onto the disk it simultaneously increases peril, decreases utility, and is wholly unsupported.

Use hardware partitions.

Viewing Partition Tables

How can you see the hardware–level partitioning used on an OpenBSD system? Use fdisk(8) for all MBR- and GPT-related tasks. The sysctl `hw.disknames` lists all of the disks installed in a system. If you run fdisk and give the disk's device node as an argument, it will show the physical partition table.

```
$ sysctl hw.disknames
hw.disknames=sd0:d25c4224901b9485,sd1:,sd2:,sd3:
```

This host has four disks, *sd0* through *sd3*. The first disk has an OpenBSD DUID assigned to it, while the others do not. That must be our boot drive. Let's take a look.

Viewing GPT Partitions

Here's a GPT partition table.

```
# fdisk sd0
Disk: sd0     Usable LBA: 34 to 1953525134 [1953525168 Sectors]
   #: type                   [         start:          size ]
---------------------------------------------------------------
   0: EFI Sys                [            64:           960 ]
   1: OpenBSD                [          1024:    1953524111 ]
```

This disk has almost two billion sectors. The "Usable LBA" entry tells us which sectors can be used by the operating system. Earlier sectors are filled by the PMBR and the GPT.

GPT partition zero is of type "EFI Sys." This is our EFI partition that contains the boot loader. It starts on sector 64 and occupies 960 sectors. You might notice some empty space between the first usable LBA and the EFI partition. OpenBSD wastes a few sectors to guarantee that any following partitions align to 4K sectors.

Partition one is of type OpenBSD. It starts in sector 1024 and runs through the rest of the disk.

An MBR looks very different.

Viewing MBR Partitions

An MBR partition table is far more complex. Disk *sd3* uses one.

```
# fdisk sd3
Disk: sd3        geometry: 121601/255/63 [1953525168 Sectors]
Offset: 0        Signature: 0xAA55
                 Starting        Ending          LBA Info:
   #: id     C   H   S -     C   H   S [ start:       size ]
---------------------------------------------------------------
   0: 00     0   0   0 -     0   0   0 [  0:            0 ] unused
   1: 00     0   0   0 -     0   0   0 [  0:            0 ] unused
   2: 00     0   0   0 -     0   0   0 [  0:            0 ] unused
  *3: A6     0   1   2 - 121601  80  63 [ 64:  1953525104 ] OpenBSD
```

First we get the disk geometry, listing the disk's cylinders, heads, and sectors per track, separated by slashes. These are all lies. Neither we nor OpenBSD have any idea what is going on inside the storage device. For the sake of understanding, let's pretend that these numbers actually mean something for a few minutes.

The *offset* is where the disk starts using sectors. Any disk you encounter today will have an offset of zero.

The disk's *signature* is a 16–bit number that uniquely identifies how this disk is used. It should always be 0xAA55, telling the hardware that this disk is bootable. That's somewhat misleading, though. If the hardware can't find a boot loader on the disk, it moves to the next disk in its list. (The boot loader not finding an operating system is a separate problem: the hardware ran the boot loader, so it is content to sit there and sneer at you. Hateful, isn't it?)

We then have the partition table. MBR partition tables must begin and end on cylinder boundaries. The exception is the first used partition, which might have a tiny bit nibbled out of it for the MBR itself. In this partition table, the first three partitions are not used. The fourth partition slot is the only one in use. The last partition is marked with an asterisk, indicating that it is active. It is of type A6, the MBR code for OpenBSD partitions. It begins on cylinder zero, head one, sector two. Sector one is the MBR. Yes, when talking about the entire disk sectors are numbered starting at zero—but in the cylinder, the count begins at one. (See why we moved to GPT?) This partition runs through the last sector of the last head of the last cylinder. For sanity's sake, the partition information in LBA format follows. Last, in case you haven't yet memorized that MBR code A6 is an OpenBSD partition, fdisk reminds us.

GPT In Detail

We've seen the basic GPT partition table, but a GPT–partitioned disk also includes a protective MBR and a secondary GPT. If you want to view all of this, add the −v flag to fdisk. Let's take a deeper look at my test system's boot disk.

```
# fdisk -v sd0
Primary GPT:
Disk: sd0    Usable LBA: 34 to 1953525134 [1953525168 Sectors]
GUID: 32761994-7611-4bce-9436-8dbe21496d60
   #: type                         [       start:         size ]
      guid                                   name
---------------------------------------------------------------
   0: EFI Sys                      [          64:          960 ]
      dc69d349-9589-4a27-b6d1-30c3e3f108ac EFI System Area
   1: OpenBSD                      [        1024:   1953524111 ]
      504926af-f37b-4412-8a32-c7f95f926394 OpenBSD Area
...
```

The output starts with a slightly more detailed view of the GPT. We see the GUID assigned to this disk, as well as the GUID for every partition.

```
Secondary GPT:
Disk: sd0    Usable LBA: 34 to 1953525134 [1953525168 Sectors]
GUID: 32761994-7611-4bce-9436-8dbe21496d60
   #: type                         [       start:         size ]
      guid                                   name
---------------------------------------------------------------
   0: EFI Sys                      [          64:          960 ]
      dc69d349-9589-4a27-b6d1-30c3e3f108ac EFI System Area
   1: OpenBSD                      [        1024:   1953524111 ]
      504926af-f37b-4412-8a32-c7f95f926394 OpenBSD Area
...
```

In theory, the secondary GPT should be identical to the primary. If it isn't, something is seriously wrong. Welcome this opportunity to test your backups.

```
MBR:
Disk: sd0        geometry: 121601/255/63 [1953525168 Sectors]
Offset: 0        Signature: 0xAA55
          Starting          Ending          LBA Info:
  #: id    C  H  S -     C   H   S [     start:          size ]
---------------------------------------------------------------------
  0: EE    0  0  2 - 121601  80  63 [      1: 1953525167 ] EFI GPT
  1: 00    0  0  0 -     0   0   0 [      0:          0 ] unused
  2: 00    0  0  0 -     0   0   0 [      0:          0 ] unused
  3: 00    0  0  0 -     0   0   0 [      0:          0 ] unused
```

The last section is the protective MBR. The PMBR claims that the disk has a single MBR partition, of type EFI. That partition's size is the largest permitted by the MBR format. If you are using this disk on hardware that does not understand GPT partitioning, this MBR will tell the hardware that the disk is partitioned. Partitioning software that only understands MBR can read this table and provide you some warning that a partition exists before you blow it away. These issues were much more common in the early days of GPT deployment, but I have faith in your ability to get yourself into a ridiculous situation where you need to know this.

Initializing Disks

When you get a new disk, it will probably have neither an MBR or a GPT. You'll need to add one. Recycled disks probably need their old partition table erased and a new one written.

OpenBSD's fdisk displays an MBR on blank disks even when no MBR is present. The only way to see that the disk is truly blank is to check the MBR signature. A signature of 0x0 means that the disk has no real MBR. You're looking at a template, not the actual MBR read from disk.

Showing a default empty MBR template is not unreasonable— you must add an MBR or a protective MBR before using the disk. It can confuse you if you have just dumped a couple megabytes from /dev/zero onto the front of your disk to obliterate the partition table, however.[7]

---

7   This is why tech authors read source code.

Creating a GPT

To create a GPT with a single partition that fills the entire disk, use the -g flag to fdisk, followed by the disk's device name.

```
# fdisk -g sd3
Do you wish to write new GPT? [n] y
```

Yes, I want to blow away everything on this disk. Enter y.

```
Writing GPT
```

This disk now has a hardware partition ready to be subdivided into OpenBSD partitions.

If a disk already has a GPT, you can blow away all existing partitions and create a single OpenBSD partition that fills the entire disk by using the -A flag. To skip the confirmation, add the -y flag.

```
# fdisk -Ay sd2
Writing GPT.
```

If you want a disk to be bootable, chances are you're installing OpenBSD on it. The simplest way to do this is to run the installer and select the target drive. Let the software do the work for you! If you really need to create a bootable GPT disk by hand, though, you must leave space for the EFI partition at the front of the disk. Do this with the -b flag, giving the size of the EFI partition in sectors as an argument. OpenBSD's standard boot loader fills 960 512-byte blocks, or a little less than half a megabyte. (OpenBSD's fdisk(8) does not respect $BLOCKSIZE, and always uses 512-byte blocks.)

```
# fdisk -A -b960 -y sd3
Writing GPT.
```

Other operating systems are less efficient with their EFI boot loaders, and need more space. Or perhaps you're playing with multibooting, and want space for a larger, more featureful bootloader. One common recommendation is a 100MB EFI partition, which requires 204,800 sectors.

```
# fdisk -Ayb 204800 sd2
```

Some operating systems have problems with oversized EFI partitions. Research your chosen operating systems' EFI tolerances before partitioning the disk.

Creating An MBR Partition

If a system doesn't recognize GPT, use MBR. To initialize a disk with a single MBR partition that covers the entire disk, use the -i flag to fdisk, followed by the disk's device name.

```
# fdisk -i sd2
Do you wish to write new MBR? [n] y
```

Yes, I want to eradicate everything on this disk. Enter y.

```
Writing MBR at offset 0.
```

You can now subdivide this hardware partition into OpenBSD partitions.

Interactive Hardware Partition Editing

You might want more complicated partitioning then simply dedicating the entire disk to OpenBSD. Don't do it.

Back in the Dark Ages, BSD systems most often used hardware partitioning to support multiple operating systems. With virtualization, this is less of an issue. If you are using software RAID, partitioning becomes important again—mostly because of hardware vendors. Disks that claim they are a particular size are not all the same size. A disk might claim to be "one terabyte," but it won't have the exact number of sectors as a different manufacturer's one terabyte disk. It might not even have the same number of blocks as a different model of one-terabyte drive from the same manufacturer. All of them are probably a tiny smidgen larger than the stated size.

Most of the time, minor size differences don't matter. If you replace a server's boot drive with one that is three megabytes smaller, partition it, reinstall the operating system, and restore your files from backup, nobody will notice those missing megabytes. If the drive was that close to full, replace it with a larger drive while you're there. Problems start when you're doing clever things like mirroring hard drives. If you replace a drive in a mirror with one that's three megabytes smaller than the smallest drive in the mirror, it flat-out won't work.

You can also do custom partitioning with fdisk's interactive mode, but that's only useful with multiboot systems. You could create physical partitions that mirror your disklabel partitions, but that adds complexity. Dedicate the entire disk to OpenBSD, and use disklabel(8) to perform partitioning.

Boot Loaders

The handoff between the hardware's boot process and the operating system is tricky. Each platform has its own protocol and requirements. A boot drive must include a *boot loader* or *boot blocks* that respect those requirements, can find the operating system, and transfer control onward. When you use the installer, OpenBSD installs the correct boot loader. If you must upgrade the boot loader after an upgrade, the release notes will inform you.

OpenBSD simplifies managing boot loaders through installboot(8). The `installboot` program identifies the hardware platform you're running on, the type of hardware partitioning on the disk, and installs the proper boot loader. All you need to do is identify the disk.

```
# installboot sd0
```

On MBR-partitioned disks, this writes all the bits needed for a successful boot to the MBR. On GPT, it formats the EFI partition and copies the necessary files there. I usually install any boot loader before creating my OpenBSD partitions.

OpenBSD Partitions

OpenBSD runs on many different hardware platforms. Some support robust and flexible partitioning schemes, like GPT. Others support limited or kludged–together schemes like MBR. Others have no concept of partitioning. A standard OpenBSD install uses nine partitions. A disk can have a maximum of sixteen partitions. How do we support these partitions on all of these different schemes?

We don't.

Hardware–specific configuration prepares portions of storage for OpenBSD, and OpenBSD divides that storage into its own partitions using the disklabel format. Whatever hardware platform you're running on, manage OpenBSD partitions via disklabels.

A disklabel maps out which blocks on a disk are assigned to which partition. Programs like newfs(8) and mount(8) read the disklabel to find partitions. Spend the time to understand disklabels early, and prevent future headaches.

Labels sound like partition tables, don't they? They do, because they are. A disklabel is a partition table. So are a GPT and an MBR. For clarity, I will refer to OpenBSD's partition tables as *disklabels* or just *labels*.

Viewing Disklabels

To see a disk's OpenBSD partitions, run disklabel(8) with the drive's device node. Here I view the label on a default OpenBSD install. We will examine the physical drive information first, and then consider the partitioning.

```
# disklabel sd0
/dev/rsd0c:
type: SCSI
disk: SCSI disk
label: Samsung SSD 870
duid: d25c4224901b9485
flags:
bytes/sector: 512
sectors/track: 63
tracks/cylinder: 255
sectors/cylinder: 16065
cylinders: 121601
total sectors: 1953525168
boundstart: 1024
boundend: 1953525135
drivedata: 0
```

This information is all read from the hardware. Changing most of it risks destabilizing your hardware.

The first entry is the raw device name, /dev/rsd0c. The leading *r* means that we are looking at a raw device node. The *sd* indicates that this is a SCSI, SATA, or other non-IDE disk, while the *0* shows that this is the first drive OpenBSD found during boot. The trailing *c* is a disklabel partition. We will look at disklabel partitions next, but the *c* partition is special. It covers the entire physical disk, and contains all other partitions.

The *type* and *disk* fields provide information about the physical disk. Historically, you might see information about IDE drives. Today, almost everything declares that it is a SCSI device and offers SCSI–compatible commands to the operating system. SATA, NVMe, USB, and almost everything else modern claims to be SCSI.

If you want information about the physical drive, the best place to look is the *label* field. Here you might find model numbers, serial numbers, or other details provided by the drive vendor. If you ever have to crack open a server containing multiple hard drives to replace one that is failing, get this information before powering off the machine. You will probably see it in minuscule print somewhere on the physical hard drive.

The *duid* field gives the DUID for this disk. OpenBSD assigns a random identifier to each disk in the system. If you ever have to replace disks, moving a cable might change drive sd2 into sd3. If your configuration files reference drives by device number, everything breaks. Refer to your drives by DUID, so hardware changes don't extend your outages.

The *flags* field provides debugging information about bad blocks or other vendor–specific details. Modern drives come with built-in spare blocks, so by the time errors appear here the drive is seriously hurting.

The fields for bytes per sector, sectors per track, tracks per cylinder, sectors per cylinder, and cylinders describe the disk's geometry. As discussed earlier, none of these numbers have anything to do with what's going on inside the drive. This virtual drive has no platters, no awareness of the underlying file system, and yet has the gall to claim a geometry.

Despite the preceding torrent of lies, the *total sectors* field is accurate.

The *boundstart* field gives the first sector you may use for disklabel partitions. Remember, blocks are numbered starting at zero. You may start partitions on this disk at block number 1024, but there are 1024 blocks before block number 1024. Similarly, *boundend* is the last sector for disklabel partitions. The total sectors might be slightly smaller than what you calculate from the drive geometry or read on the vendor's packaging.

The *drivedata* field contains other information read from the drive. I have not seen this field populated on any modern drive.

We then have actual partition information.

```
16 partitions:
#              size      offset   fstype [fsize bsize   cpg]
  a:        2097152        1024   4.2BSD  2048 16384 12960 # /
  b:       66134304     2098176     swap                   # none
  c:     1953525168           0   unused
  d:        8388608    68232480   4.2BSD  2048 16384 12960 # /tmp
  e:      139608640    76621088   4.2BSD  2048 16384 12960 # /var
  f:       12582912   216229728   4.2BSD  2048 16384 12960 # /usr
  g:        2097152   228812640   4.2BSD  2048 16384 12960 # /usr/X11R6
  h:       41943040   230909792   4.2BSD  2048 16384 12960 # /usr/local
  i:            960          64    MSDOS
  j:        6291456   272852832   4.2BSD  2048 16384 12960 # /usr/src
  k:       12582912   279144288   4.2BSD  2048 16384 12960 # /usr/obj
  l:      629145536   291727232   4.2BSD  4096 32768 26062 # /home
```

This disklabel supports up to sixteen partitions, but only twelve are configured. Hash marks indicate comments.

The first column is the partition letter. Each partition has a letter *a* through *p*. Unused partitions are not shown. On a boot drive, partition *a* is always the root filesystem and partition *b* is the swap space. If you look at a non-boot drive, these letters might be assigned to any partition. The OpenBSD installer assigns partition letters as it sees fit.

The second column gives the partition size in blocks. On this drive partition *a* fills 2097152 blocks, partition *b* 66134304 blocks, and partition *c* 1953525168 blocks.

The third column, the *offset*, is the number of blocks from the beginning of the disk where the disklabel partition begins. Partition *a* has an offset of 64. If you look back at the `boundstart` field, you'll see that the first block we can use is block 1024. This is the first partition on the disk.

Look at partition *b*. It has an offset of 2,098,176. If you add the size of partition *a* and its offset, you will see that they also add up to (2,097,152+1024=) 2,098,176. Partition *b* begins in the sector immediately after partition *a* ends. Understanding partitioning is pure second-grade addition, except the numbers are inconveniently large for our feeble brains.

This all seems straightforward until we look at partition *c*. It has an offset of zero and is as large as all of the other partitions combined. Partition c represents the entire disk. You cannot put a file system on partition *c*, it exists only for reference. Partition *d* begins right after the end of partition *b*.

The next column, *fstype*, gives the file system on this partition. OpenBSD UFS partitions are of type *4.2BSD*. If your disk uses GPT, you will also see an *MSDOS* partition for the EFI boot loader. Swap space has type *swap*.

The next two columns give the file system fragment size and block size. OpenBSD's disklabel bases UFS fragment and block sizes on the partition's size. We discuss UFS blocks and fragments in chapter 2.

The *cpg* column tells us the number of cylinders per cylinder group in this file system. This is entirely about keeping track of the disk's lies. Ignore it.

Finally, we have a comment telling us where the file system should be mounted.

Physical Partitions and Disklabels

Take a close look at partition *i*. In amidst all of these orderly partitions that proceed one after the other, this partition has an offset of 64 and a size of 960. It's before even our root partition. This disk uses GPT partitioning, and this partition is our EFI.

When you create an OpenBSD disklabel, it pulls in any recognized physical partitions and adds them to the disklabel. Access the GPT's EFI partition as `/dev/sd0i` without any tedious mucking about with different device nodes or slices or similar abstractions other operating systems need.

This disklabel entry is a convenience for the sysadmin. Editing this disklabel entry won't change the GPT partition. To change the physical partitioning, use fdisk(8).

These partitions are created when the disk is first labeled. If you remove the entry, disklabel won't recreate it for you. If you add new fdisk partitions, they will not get automatically added to the label.

Editing Disklabels

Let's take one of those blank disks and put some partitions on it. Don't leap headfirst into the partition editor, though. Make a plan. Write it down. Think before you partition.

This host will be a MariaDB server. Drive `sd1` is four terabytes. A check with fdisk(8) verifies that it has been partitioned with a single GPT partition.

```
# fdisk sd1
Disk: sd1   Usable LBA: 34 to 7814037134 [7814037168 Sectors]
   #: type       [        start:          size ]
--------------------------------------------------------------
   0: OpenBSD    [           64:     7814037071 ]
```

I will allocate the first gigabyte to an alternate root partition (`/altroot`). The next 65GB will be allocated to swap, in case I add more memory to this host and must dump a kernel panic. (Chapter 3 discusses swap.) I will use 2 TB for a `/var/mysql` partition. The remaining space gets dumped into a `/scratch` partition, which I can use for random tasks that need space.

The disklabel(8) program provides a menu-driven editor and direct text editing. The menu-driven method lets you add and remove partitions easily, prevents overlapping partitions and other daft errors, and performs the math for you. The text editor method lets you drown in failure. We'll stick with the menus.

Enter the menu-driven editor with the −E flag. Specify the drive you want to work on.

```
# disklabel -E sd1
Label editor (enter '?' for help at any prompt)
sd1>
```

The editor copies the current label into memory. Any changes you make happen to the copy, not the original. When you finish editing and are satisfied with your new label, write the new label to the disk. If you mess up your new label, exit the editor without writing it to disk and start over.

In case you forget where you are and what you're doing, the prompt reminds you of the disk you're mucking with.

View the Label

Use the p command to print the in-memory copy of the label.

```
sd1> p
OpenBSD area: 64-7814037135; size: 7814037071; free: 7814037071
#                size           offset  fstype [fsize bsize   cpg]
  c:       7814037168              0  unused
```

This disk is blank. Remember, the *c* partition represents the entire disk. That's a lot of blocks to count without even commas to break it up, so you can show the size by adding a k for KB, m for MB, g for GB, or t for TB. You must put a space between the *p* and the size. If you use an asterisk, disklabel uses the unit suitable for the smallest partition.

```
sd1> p *
OpenBSD area: 64-7814037135; size: 3.6T; free: 3.6T
#                size           offset  fstype [fsize bsize   cpg]
  c:             3.6T              0  unused
```

This drive has 3.6 terabytes of space for partitions.[8] Let's make some.

---

[8] "When is a 3.6 TB drive a 4 TB drive?"

"When you read the vendor packaging."

Creating Partitions

Before doing anything, review the plan.

- 1 GB /altroot
- 65 GB swap
- 2TB /var/mysql
- everything else in /scratch

Use the a command to add a partition. We'll start with our
/altroot.

```
sd1> a
partition: [a]
offset: [64]
size: [7814037071] 1g
FS type: [4.2BSD]
sd1*>
```

First we're prompted for the *partition* letter. OpenBSD defaults to alphabetical order. For many people, that's fine. I'm easily confused, so I reserve *a* for root-like partitions and *b* for swap space. This partition is for my new */altroot*, so I hit ENTER to take the default.

The *offset* is the block where the partition begins. Look back at our fdisk output, and you'll see that 64 is the beginning of our OpenBSD physical partition. The editor provides a sensible default. Change it and you'll have to do second grade math with large numbers. Again, take the default.

The *size* defaults to "the rest of the disk." Enter the size you want here. You can use the k, m, g, and t abbreviations rather than blocks.

Finally, the *FS type* lets you enter either 4.2BSD or swap. We'll discuss RAID in Chapter 7.

When you return to the editor command prompt, note the asterisk added to the disk name. This indicates that the editor has changes that are not yet saved to disk.

Repeat the process for the new swap partition.

```
sd1*> a
partition: [b]
offset: [2215168]
size: [7811821967] 65g
FS type: [swap]
```

This is almost the same, except for the new partition letters and smaller default size. The editor knows that partition *b* is traditionally swap space, so it sets the default filesystem type to swap.

Create the /var/mysql partition.

```
sd1*> a
partition: [d]
offset: [138644520]
size: [7675392615] 2t
FS type: [4.2BSD]
```

The editor knows that *c* is taken, and skips to *d*.

The /scratch partition will use all the remaining space, so you can just take the defaults everywhere.

Check your work. I add the g flag to show size in gigabytes instead of blocks.

```
sd1*> p g
OpenBSD area: 64-7814037135; size: 3726.0G; free: 0.0G
#                size        offset  fstype [fsize bsize    cpg]
  a:             1.1G            64  4.2BSD   2048 16384  12960
  b:            65.1G       2215168    swap
  c:          3726.0G             0  unused
  d:          2048.0G     138644608  4.2BSD   8192 65536  52270
  e:          1611.9G    4433627520  4.2BSD   8192 65536  52270
```

This looks good. Let's write it to disk.

Finalizing or Discarding Labels

Your edited disklabel is either correct, or trash. Save your finished label and exit the editor with q.

```
sd1*> q
Write new label?: [y] y
```

You get one last chance to change your mind. Enter y to confirm. The editors writes the label to disk and exits.

Use the w command to write the label but remain in the editor.

The x command exits the editor without saving any changes to disk.

The label now includes the partitions. Swap partitions are immediately usable. Before using data partitions you must create a filesystem and mount them, as discussed in Chapter 2.

Other Editor Commands

The u command undoes the most recent change. If you use u twice in a row, it re-does the change.

To throw away all your changes and read the disk's actual label back into memory, use U.

If you want a reminder of the editor commands, enter ? or h. For an in-depth reminder, hit M to print the disklabel(8) man page.

If you are a filesystem expert and want to muck with disk geometry or block and fragment size, you can enter expert mode with X. Most sysadmins should never use this option.

Label Backup, Restore, and Duplication

You can copy disk labels to a text file, and use that text file to restore the label. This lets you recover from a botched editing job, or duplicate the partitioning on another disk. Here I grab the disklabel from drive sd2.

```
# disklabel sd2 > /tmp/sd2.disklabel
```

If you want to copy the disklabel as you're editing, use the s command. Give it one argument, the text file to copy the label to. If you don't give a filename, the editor prompts you for one.

```
# disklabel -E sd2
Label editor (enter '?' for help at any prompt)
sd2> s /tmp/sd2.disklabel
sd2> q
No label changes.
```

Now that you have the disklabel saved to a file, you can label a disk of the same size or larger from that file using the −R flag.

```
# disklabel -R disk file
```

My disks *sd2* and *sd3* are identical. If I want to label disk *sd3* using the label from disk *sd2*, I would run this command.

```
# disklabel -R sd3 /tmp/sd2.disklabel
```

The partitioning is written to the disk.

You can put a label from a smaller disk on a larger disk, but you cannot use a label from a large drive on a smaller drive.

Modifying Disklabels

Over time, my MariaDB databases grow and the database partition becomes uncomfortably full. I want to remove the */scratch* partition and add that space to the */var/mysql* partition. Any time you touch a disk with existing data partitions, verify your backups before doing *anything*. Also back up the current disklabel before making any edits.

You cannot modify a mounted partition's label entry; it must be unmounted before you can change it. If a label has multiple partitions, you can leave the partitions you're not using mounted.

```
# disklabel -E sd1
Label editor (enter '?' for help at any prompt)
```

Check the current partition table.

```
sd1> p
OpenBSD area: 64-7814037135; size: 7814037071; free: 103
#                size       offset  fstype [fsize bsize    cpg]
  a:          2215104           64  4.2BSD    2048 16384 12960
  b:        136429352      2215168    swap
  c:       7814037168            0  unused
  d:       4294982912    138644608  4.2BSD    8192 65536 52270
  e:       3380409600   4433627520  4.2BSD    8192 65536 52270
```

Partition *d* is for */var/mysql*, while partition *e* is */scratch*. I want to delete partition *e* and add its space to partition *d*.

Use the d command to delete a partition. Here, I delete *e*.

```
sd1> d e
```

That's it. My `/scratch` partition no longer exists on the in-memory label.

```
sd1*> p
OpenBSD area: 64-7814037135; size: 7814037071; free:
3380409703
#                size        offset  fstype [fsize bsize    cpg]
  a:          2215104            64  4.2BSD    2048 16384 12960
  b:        136429352       2215168    swap
  c:       7814037168             0  unused
  d:       4294982912     138644608  4.2BSD    8192 65536 52270
```

The editor's label has no partition *e*, and the disk has a bunch of free space. We are on the way.

Now modify partition *d* with the m command. Give the partition letter as an argument.

```
sd1*> m d
offset: [138644608]
size: [4294982912] *
FS type: [4.2BSD]
sd1*>
```

The presented defaults are all the partition's existing values. I don't want to change the partition's *offset*; it still begins in the same place.

I want to change the *size*. The partition currently fills 4294982912 blocks, shown as the default, and I want to assign the rest of the disk to it. Rather than digging up exact values, I can use an asterisk (*) to indicate the rest of the disk.

Converting this filesystem to swap would be counterproductive, so I leave the filesystem type alone. The label now looks like so.

```
sd1*> p g
OpenBSD area: 64-7814037135; size: 3726.0G; free: 0.0G
#                size        offset  fstype [fsize bsize    cpg]
  a:             1.1G            64  4.2BSD    2048 16384 12960
  b:            65.1G       2215168    swap
  c:          3726.0G             0  unused
  d:          3659.9G     138644608  4.2BSD    8192 65536 52270
```

The *d* partition has been increased from 2TB to over three and a half. That gives me plenty of time to get a new, larger disk. Write the new label to disk.

```
sd1*> q
```

Congratulations, you now have a larger partition. If you mount that partition, though, you'll notice something odd.

```
# df -h
...
/dev/sd1d      2.0T     1.9T     64G     97%     /var/mysql
```

Our partition is three and a half terabytes, so why does it show as being only two?

A filesystem lives on a partition, but is a separate thing. Once you increase the size of a partition, you must use growfs(8) to make the filesystem larger as discussed in Chapter 3.

Even at this point, your changes are not irrevocable. You haven't written anything to the blocks previously allocated to */scratch*. If you restore the old disklabel from the backup file, the deleted sd1e and your */scratch* filesystem will miraculously reappear. Expanding another filesystem into those blocks will overwrite data.

Erasing Labels

Sometimes you need to recycle a disk, discarding an old irrelevant partition table and starting anew. While you could go into the label editor and manually delete all the partitions, there are easier ways.

If you're in the editor, z removes all partitions. You could also use the d command with an asterisk.

You can also start the editor with a default disklabel, ignoring the existing label, by adding the −d flag. The default label is useful because it includes other physical partitions, such as the EFI partition. Disk *sd3* has a label, but here I ignore it to start with a default label.

```
# disklabel -d -E sd3
Label editor (enter '?' for help at any prompt)
sd3> p
OpenBSD area: 204864-1953525135; size: 1953320271; free: 1953320271
#                size              offset  fstype [fsize bsize    cpg]
  c:        1953525168                 0   unused
  i:            204800                64   MSDOS
```

Partition *i* is the EFI GPT partition.

Customizing Label Headers

We've spent most of our efforts on partitioning disks, but you can also alter certain fields in the top of the label by directly editing the label. This isn't worth the effort for small systems, but if you have a large storage array with many disks it's invaluable. The kernel error *drive sd97 is dying* is useless unless you can attach that error to a specific piece of hardware.

Before editing a label, copy the label to a file so that when you mess up you can restore it. Now fire up disklabel with the −e flag.

disklabel -e sd1

This brings up the disklabel in a text editor, including the partition table and the informational fields at the top. Let's look at the top of the label header.

```
# /dev/rsd0c:
type: SCSI
disk: SCSI disk
label: Samsung SSD 870
duid: d25c4224901b9485
flags:
bytes/sector: 512
...
```

OpenBSD uses everything below the DUID for disk and filesystem management, involving actual math. Tamper with them at your peril. The comment indicating where the drive was attached when the label was written and the disk type are immutable. You can change the disk, label, and duid fields, however.

The disk should indicate what kind of disk this is, but these days everything uses the SCSI interface. You can put identifying information here.

The label is a sixteen-character string initialized by reading from the drive. If you have a large storage array where you have to swap out disks, it might make sense to put a physical label with an inventory number on the drive and put the inventory number on the drive label. An error message on disk *sd97* triggers a check of that drive's

49

disklabel, which gives you the number on the drive so you can have an underpaid flunky hunt through the storage array until they find it.

Changing the disk `duid` is tempting. Why use gibberish sixteen-digit hexadecimal strings when you could call the disk `0000000000000001`? That works fine, until you have to move a drive from one host to another. You might think you'll never do that, but I've lost count of the number of times I've put a dead machine's drive into a USB adapter to retrieve a file. If you must use custom DUIDs, give each machine a short hexadecimal name and put that at the front of the DUID, then number the disks at the end. A DUID like `badc0decafe00005` works fine.

If you have duplicate DUIDs in the same machine, OpenBSD recognizes none of them. A Disk Unique Identifier that is not unique is not a DUID.

Now that you can cope with partitions, let's put some filesystems on them.

"Many users assume that their advanced filesystem is better than UFS because they have so many features— snapshots, checksums, compression, sophisticated caching algorithms, and so on—while all UFS has ever done is muck about putting data on disk. But, conversely, UFS users believe their filesystem is better for exactly the same reasons."

—Hitchhikers Guide to OpenBSD

Chapter 2: the Unix File System

OpenBSD's primary filesystem, the Unix File System (UFS), is a direct descendant of the filesystem shipped with primordial BSD. It has undergone literal decades of debugging and tuning, and is considered robust and reliable. OpenBSD is not the only operating system that uses a filesystem rooted in BSD—if a vendor does not tout its "miraculous filesystem," it's almost certainly running a UFS derivative. UFS is designed to trivially support the most common situations easily, while giving you the flexibility to cope with weirdness.

UFS is tightly integrated with the OpenBSD kernel, even in places you might not expect it like the virtual memory stack and support for non-UFS filesystems. Wherever you look, you'll find UFS concepts. Understanding the basics of UFS is critical to OpenBSD administration.

The original UFS was written in the 1980s and included sensible hard-coded limits, like a maximum filesystem size just under one terabyte. Who would possibly spend the millions of dollars on a disk that large anyway? Today we use UFS2, which overwhelmingly uses the same logic but increases a bunch of 32-bit values to 64 bits. No, it wasn't as easy as changing the size of all the variables. Yes, early adopters had entire filesystems sent to sleep with the fishes.

Today, UFS2 is solid and reliable. It's the default filesystem on all of OpenBSD's modern platforms. Older platforms still use UFS, generally called UFS1 for clarity. We will focus on UFS2.

UFS Components

UFS is built in two layers, the Unix File System and the Fast File System (FFS). People tend to use the names interchangeably, but each has a specific role. UFS handles user-visible tasks like filenames and directories and the connections between them, permissions, and so on. FFS does the ugly work of efficiently getting files onto disk in a way that makes them quickly accessible, so that when it must find and read a file it can do so efficiently. Decades of development have intertwined the two so thoroughly that they're probably inseparable today, however. When someone talks about the innards of UFS, they're probably discussing FFS.

So let's talk about the innards of UFS—er, FFS. FFS is built out of blocks, fragments, and inodes.

A *block* is a piece of disk that contains data. (The word "block" is still ambiguous, but I attempt to reserve it for filesystem blocks whenever possible.) Filesystem blocks fill multiple disk sectors. While each UFS filesystem can have its own block size, 16KB is a common size. If you have a 64KB file, it fills four filesystem blocks.

Not all files are even multiples of a block size, so UFS stores the leftover bits in *fragments*. A fragment is one-eighth of the block size. If you have 16KB blocks, each fragment is 2KB. A 19KB file would be stuffed into one block and one fragment, wasting 1KB. Without fragments, this file would use two blocks and waste 5KB. When UFS needs more fragments, it allocates a block for them.

UFS keeps track of its files by allocating certain blocks as *inodes*, or *index nodes*. An inode contains each file's size, permissions, and the list of blocks and fragments each file uses. Inode data is collectively called *metadata*. Inodes are allocated at filesystem creation, proportional to the filesystem size. A modern disk probably has hundreds of thousands of inodes on each filesystem, enough to support tens of thousands of files. While UFS is generous in allocating inodes, a specialty filesystem with a huge number of very tiny files might need extra inodes. Use df -i to see how many inodes your filesystem has used. You cannot add inodes to an existing filesystem; to get more inodes, you must recreate the filesystem.

All this gets glued together with the *superblock*, a master index of filesystem characteristics. It contains the magic number that identifies the filesystem as OpenBSD UFS, as well as geometry information used to optimize reading and writing files. Every UFS filesystem maintains many copies of the superblock, in case the primary gets damaged.

OpenBSD's FFS reserves five percent of every filesystem for scratch space, letting it defragment itself and move files and perform other housekeeping tasks. This lets it focus on working as quickly as possible during interactive tasks, while cleaning up after itself in otherwise idle time. You can overfill a filesystem, cutting into that reserved space, but FFS immediately switches its attention to cramming every file onto the disk as tightly as possibly. Performance plunges.

UFS has roots in the early age of BSD, when storage geometry was vital and the sysadmin could expect to know exactly what was happening inside the disk. Modern UFS, however, doesn't rely so much on disk geometry. It mostly ignores cylinders and tracks and heads. The one geometry UFS recognizes is cylinder groups, but that's not because of anything special about the disks. UFS needs a basic metadata structure, including a list of blocks that belong to that metadata, and cylinder groups were right there. Changing UFS to be a geometry-free filesystem would only replace cylinder groups with another made-up thing.

Filesystem Mounts

Attaching a filesystem to the directory tree is called *mounting*. OpenBSD provides many ways to fine-tune filesystem mounts, but we'll start with the basics. To see what is currently mounted, run mount(8) without any arguments.

```
# mount
/dev/sd0a on / type ffs (local)
/dev/sd0l on /home type ffs (local, nodev, nosuid)
/dev/sd0d on /tmp type ffs (local, nodev, nosuid)
/dev/sd0f on /usr type ffs (local, nodev)
...
```

You'll see the device node and the mount point. After that we get the filesystem type. Both UFS1 and UFS2 partitions are displayed as type *ffs*. Any filesystem-specific mount options are shown afterwards, in parenthesis. The word *local* indicates that this is a local filesystem, on a disk physically attached to this host.

Adding the −v option gives you the DUID used to mount the filesystem, as well as the change time for the mount. For most mounts, the change time is when the partition was mounted.

Where does OpenBSD learn what to mount, and where? From the filesystem table.

/etc/fstab

The file /etc/fstab contains the host's filesystem table. Filesystems described in this table can be easily or automatically mounted, while mounting other filesystems requires more complicated commands. The filesystem table describes which filesystems should be mounted, where they should be mounted, the mount options, and when to run backups and check the filesystem's integrity. Each filesystem appears on a single line, as shown here.

```
d25c4224901b9485.b none swap sw
d25c4224901b9485.a / ffs rw 1 1
d25c4224901b9485.l /home ffs rw,nodev,nosuid 1 2
...
```

The first field gives the filesystem's location, most often by the disk's DUID and the partition letter. The first partition in this table is `d25c4224901b9485.b`, the second is `d25c4224901b9485.a`, and so on. It is possible to use device nodes instead, like `sd0a`, but the device node might change if the hardware finds the drives in a different order at boot. Partition `sd1b` could become `sd0b` at the next boot, and get used for swap—an especially amusing error if that's your database.

The second field gives the mount point. The first entry has a mount point of `none`, so it does not get attached to the directory tree. The second entry has a mount point of /—it's the root partition. The third entry is for `/home`.

The third field offers the filesystem type. The first entry is of type `swap`, so it's swap space. The second and third entries are of type `ffs`, so they are UFS.

The following field offers the mount options. We'll learn about the different mount options later this chapter. Swap space is always mounted with the option *sw*. Our root partition has the *rw* mount option. The home partition has the *rw,* *nodev*, and *nosuid* options. Note that there is no space after these commas. The mount options must contain one of `rw`, `ro`, or `sw`, or mount(8) won't recognize the mount point. (The alternate roots discussed later this chapter use the `xx` mount option. It's not a valid mount option, but alternate roots should not be routinely mounted.)

For UFS filesystems, the next number indicates if dump(8) should back up the filesystem. The dump program is the primordial UFS backup, so the filesystem table gives it special consideration. If you're still using dump(8), give a backup level here.

The last field is the *pass number*. It tells fsck(8) when to verify the filesystem during boot. Filesystems with a pass number of 1 are verified first, those with 2 are verified second, and so on. A pass number of 0, or no pass number at all, tells fsck to skip validating this filesystem. We'll talk about fsck(8) later this chapter.

Mount Options

People trying to violate a system do strange things, and some of those things involve filesystems. A user who can create and access device nodes in their home directory might be able to get extra access to those devices. If someone can compile their own software and make it setuid, they could get extra access. The list of tricks people have successfully used is longer than this entire book.

OpenBSD uses mount options to enforce security policies. If the operating system doesn't recognize setuid programs or device nodes in user-writable directories, that eliminates entire classes of attack. It also helps stabilize the system against accidental d amage. Every experienced sysadmin, at some point, asked "what does this button do" and discovered the answer was "something undesirable." Mount options stop the most egregious bad things.

Many of these mount options are mutually exclusive. You cannot mount a filesystem both read-write and read-only. If options conflict, the last one wins.

Here are OpenBSD's mount options, as you might encounter in `/etc/fstab`. Some are FFS-only, while others apply to any filesystem.

Read-Write Mounts

To both read and write to the filesystem, mount it *read-write*. When you first install OpenBSD, it mounts all partitions read-write.

Read-write mounts are the default. To explicitly configure them, use the `rw` option.

Read-Only Mounts

If you want the system to be able to read a filesystem's contents, but never write to it or change it in any way, use a *read-only* mount. A filesystem that cannot be changed cannot be corrupted.

Read-only mounts are also valuable when trying to access a damaged filesystem. OpenBSD won't let you perform a read-write mount on a corrupt filesystem, but by mounting them read-only you have a chance of recovering some data from the filesystem.

To mount a filesystem read-only, use the option `ro`, `rdonly`, or `norw`.

Synchronous Mounts

A *synchronous* mount is the safest and the slowest way to mount a filesystem. OpenBSD reads data from synchronously mounted partition as fast as the hardware permits. Whenever you write to the disk, however, the kernel feeds a morsel of data to the disk, waits to receive confirmation that the disk has accepted the data and written it to the disk, and then informs the writing program that the write is complete. There is no optimization. Synchronous mounts are written very slowly.

Synchronous mounts are not as safe as you might think, though. The sooner you internalize that *all storage devices lie*, the less miserable you will be. Benchmarks motivate drive manufacturers to report data as written to disk as quickly as possible, when perhaps the writes are cached in a secondary storage medium. This means that your synchronous mount isn't truly synchronous, only more synchronous than other sorts of mounts. You might use them when data integrity is paramount but most of the time, they're overkill.

The `sync` option enables synchronous mounts.

Asynchronous Mounts

If the storage device's lies are inadequate, you can get your kernel to join in the lies using *asynchronous* mounts. When given data to write to an asynchronously-mounted filesystem, the kernel immediately reports that the write was successful. The drive doesn't even get a chance to respond. Asynchronous mounts are fast, but risk data corruption.

Asynchronous mounts are useful when restoring filesystems from backup, though. If the power dies halfway through the restore, you'll need to start over anyway. Don't use asynchronous mounts in production unless you don't mind your data getting sucked away to an alternate dimension.

The *async* option enables asynchronous mounts.

Soft Update Mounts

Soft updates are an FFS optimization that arranges disk writes so that the filesystem's metadata remains consistent at all times. This gives performance approaching that of an asynchronous mount with the reliability of a synchronous mount. A power failure at the wrong instant will still lose data, but soft updates prevent most filesystem integrity problems. You might still need fsck(8) to recover, but any errors can be automatically corrected.

Soft updates do not convert FFS into a journaling filesystem. While metadata management has a passing similarity to certain types of journaling, the similarity is only superficial.

So what's the downside? Soft updates reorder writes so that the filesystem can't ever be inconsistent. If you reorder writes, for every byte that gets written more quickly, another byte is delayed. It uses a little more memory than standard read-write mounts.

Should you use soft updates? That depends. If an automatic fsck(8) fails, can you manually repair a filesystem with fsdb(8) and clri(8)? After decades of using FFS, I can't. Are you running on a tiny system with minuscule memory? If the answers to both are no, and you're using a modern amd64 system, I recommend soft updates.

Use the option `softdep` to activate soft updates.

"Don't Track Access Time" Mounts

FFS records the last time a file was read, storing it as a file's `atime`. Updating these access times consumes a measurable amount of disk throughput. If you don't need these access times, disable them.

Using noatime is often sensible on desktops and laptops, where minimizing power usage is critical. If you're tempted to use this option on a server, buy a faster disk instead. Some software, like the Mutt mail client, use atime to perform basic functions and won't work properly on atime-free filesystems.

Stop tracking access time with the `noatime` option.

Device Nodes Forbidden Mounts

With rare exceptions, device nodes belong only in */dev*. Intruders might try to create rogue device nodes elsewhere and use them to attack the host, but if the kernel won't recognize those device nodes this whole category of attacks fails.

Rejecting device nodes on a filesystem is also useful if you multiboot your host. If you dual-boot OpenBSD and Linux, you don't want to accidentally access a device node from the wrong operating system.

Use the `nodev` option to ignore device nodes on a filesystem. By default, OpenBSD forbids device nodes everywhere but */dev*.

Execution Forbidden Mounts

Some filesystems should not normally contain executable programs. If you're running a web server, users don't need to go compiling programs in their home directories. Telling the kernel to ignore executables on certain filesystems prevents users from running their own programs. You'll also need to forbid executables on shared space like */tmp* and */var/tmp*.

Forbidding execution of binaries doesn't stop scripts, though. Shell scripts execute from */bin/sh*, and Perl from */usr/bin/perl*. It will slow intruders down, however, and users will have to make distinct efforts to break policy.

Use the `noexec` option to forbid execution on a filesystem.

setuid Forbidden Mounts

A setuid program can run as a different user. These programs present security issues, and should be installed only by the system administrator. OpenBSD disables setuid programs everywhere except */usr* by default. If you add new filesystems, you should disable setuid there as well.

Use the `nosuid` option to disable setuid programs.

Allow Read-Write-Execute Memory

In theory, a running program should be stored in a section of read-only but executable memory. The binary for ls(1) should not rewrite itself as it runs. It should also have a section of read-write but nonexecutable memory, for doing its work. This requires careful programming, however. Many programs declare "give me some read-write-executable memory" and start shuffling pointers everywhere. Intruders take advantage of this weakness to corrupt running programs.

OpenBSD's core programs allocate separate read-execute and read-write memory. Programs that ask for writable and executable memory are automatically killed. Many popular third-party programs are not so carefully programmed, however. Using these programs requires lifting that restriction.

The `wxallowed` option disables this protection for programs on a particular filesystem. It is normally used only on */usr/local*.

Forcibly Mount

You have a corrupt filesystem? Cool. You insist on mounting it read-write, even though it will probably corrupt your kernel? Well, it's a learning experience. You could clean the filesystem before mounting it, as discussed later this chapter, but some people like to go skinny-dipping in the shark tank.

Use the `force` option to mount a corrupt filesystem.

Do Not Automatically Mount This Filesystem

This isn't so much a mount option as an instruction for the filesystem table. OpenBSD tries to mount every filesystem listed in */etc/fstab* at boot. Any filesystem listed there can easily be mounted and unmounted. If a filesystem in */etc/fstab* is missing, the boot will hang. That's fine, until you want to create an */etc/fstab* entry for removable media or an NFS server. You don't want a boot to hang because you didn't plug in a flash drive!

Use the *noauto* option in */etc/fstab* to tell OpenBSD to not try to mount this filesystem at boot. The boot will proceed normally, and later you can run *mount /usb* to get at your flash drive.

Disregard Filesystem Permissions

When can regular users create files owned by `root`? When the filesystem is mounted to allow such.

Permission-free mounts are intended to allow unprivileged users to build OpenBSD releases. The user can build and install privileged binaries and device nodes in a chrooted filesystem without privileged access to the host. The kernel won't execute any binaries on such a filesystem, and ignores any device nodes. The permissions on the mount point control who may access and alter the permissions-free filesystem.

Disregard permissions, executables, and device nodes with the `noperm` mount option.

Most folks have no need for this option, but people always want to know more than is healthy, so here you go.

What's Mounted Now

If your host has been running for longer than it takes to make a cup of tea, the filesystems might have changed. To see the current state of your host's filesystems, run mount(8) without any options.

```
$ mount
/dev/sd0a on / type ffs (local)
/dev/sd0l on /home type ffs (local, nodev, nosuid)
/dev/sd0d on /tmp type ffs (local, nodev, nosuid)
/dev/sd0f on /usr type ffs (local, nodev)
/dev/sd0g on /usr/X11R6 type ffs (local, nodev)
/dev/sd0h on /usr/local type ffs (local, nodev, wxallowed)
/dev/sd0k on /usr/obj type ffs (local, nodev, nosuid)
/dev/sd0j on /usr/src type ffs (local, nodev, nosuid)
/dev/sd0e on /var type ffs (local, nodev, nosuid)
/dev/sd0i on /efi type msdos (local)
```

All currently mounted partitions appear. You see the device node, the mount point, and the filesystem type. The mount options (discussed later this chapter) appear in parentheses. Most of these filesystems are of type ffs, but some doofus who needed an example of a non-FFS filesystem mounted the EFI boot loader at /efi.[9]

---

[9]   Yes, you can mount the EFI partition and have a good rummage. Wise people use a read-only mount.

Mounting and Unmounting Filesystems

Access a filesystem by attaching it to the directory tree with mount(8). If you've never mounted filesystems by hand before, boot your test machine into single-user mode and follow along.

The root partition is the root of the directory tree; without it, no other filesystem can be accessed. Identifying the partition containing the root filesystem is a key part of OpenBSD's boot process. In single-user mode, the root filesystem is the only one mounted. It contains just enough of the system to establish a shell and mount other filesystems. On a host freshly booted into single-user mode, go look in /usr. It's empty. The filesystem isn't mounted.

To do any real work in single-user mode, you probably need to mount other filesystems.

Mounting Filesystems in /etc/fstab

To mount a filesystem listed in /etc/fstab, give mount(8) the filesystem's mount point. While running in single-user mode, here I mount /usr and /var.

```
# mount /usr
# mount /var
```

This parses /etc/fstab, grabs the filesystems, and mounts them exactly as described.

To mount all the local filesystems listed in /etc/fstab, except for the ones flagged noauto, use mount's -a flag.

```
# mount -a
```

You can now get at your files.

Remounting Filesystems

Suppose a system configuration error prevents a host from booting into multi-user mode. This could be a goof in /etc/rc.conf.local, or /etc/mygate, or even /etc/fstab. You need to boot into single-user mode, fix the goof, and reboot. These critical files are usually in /etc,

62

on the root partition. But if you boot into single-user mode and check the root partition, you'll see this.

```
# mount
root_device on / type ffs (local, read-only)
```

Changing files requires a read-write mount. If you mount all of your filesystems with `mount -a`, it automatically updates the root partition to a read-write mount. If one of the filesystems is damaged, you might not have that luxury. Update a partition's mount options with `-u`, specifying the mount options with `-o` exactly as in `/etc/fstab`. Here, I want the root filesystem to be mounted read-write, with soft updates.

```
# mount -u -o rw,softdep /
```

The root mount point is updated. I can make the necessary changes. The reverse is slightly more complicated. You can't update a filesystem from a read-write mount to a read-only mount unless it has no files open for writing.

You can use mount `-u` to change other mount options, but most of the time such changes are best made in `/etc/fstab` and tested with a reboot. Doing otherwise is how you get unbootable systems.

Unmounting Filesystems

There is no unmount(8) command. It's umount(8), with only one *n*. To disconnect a filesystem from the directory tree, give it one argument, the mount point to be disconnected. Here I unmount my `/test` partition.

```
# umount /test
```

You cannot unmount filesystems that a program is using. Even an idle command prompt in a directory will prevent you from disconnecting the filesystem.

To unmount everything except the root partition, use the `-a` flag.

```
# umount -a
```

This makes most sense in single-user mode, when followed by a mount -a for testing /etc/fstab changes.

Mounting Filesystems Without /etc/fstab

Suppose you've partitioned a new disk and created filesystems, and want to test-mount them before making /etc/fstab entries. Or maybe you've added a new disk to replace an existing filesystem, but need to mount the old filesystem at a temporary location to copy files over. Give mount(8) two arguments, the device node and the mount point.

```
# mount /dev/sd2d /scratch
```

You could also use the disk DUID to mount the partition. I manually assigned a legible DUID to this disk.

```
# mount badc0decafe00001.d /scratch
```

Verify it's there with mount(8).

```
# mount
...
/dev/sd2d on /scratch type ffs (local)
```

Use the -o flag to add any options. This partition isn't quite disposable enough to mount async, but I do want soft updates and noatime. I don't want device nodes or setuid binaries on it either.

```
# mount -o softdep,noatime,nodev,nosuid badc0decafe00001.d /scratch
```

Depending on what I want this scratch space used for, I might also want noexec.

Creating UFS Filesystems

Use newfs(8) to build an UFS filesystem on a partition. The newfs(8) command requires one argument: either the full path to the partition's raw device node (such as /dev/rsd3d), or the partition's block device without the path (sd3d).

```
# newfs /dev/rsd3d
/dev/rsd3d: 953869.6MB in 1953525056 sectors of 512 bytes
292 cylinder groups of 3266.88MB, 52270 blocks, 104704 inodes each
super-block backups (for fsck -b #) at:
 256, 6690816, 13381376, 20071936, 26762496,…
```

You'll see details about the filesystem's size, how many disk sectors it uses, and so on. It assumes each disk sector is 512 bytes, which is not the same as the size of the filesystem blocks or fragments.

As newfs(8) marches along, it prints the location of each superblock. This is leftover from the days when computers and disks were much slower, and served as a progress bar. If you silence these with the -q argument and build a filesystem on a fast drive, you might get the impression that it takes longer to print these messages on your screen than to build the filesystem.

Viewing UFS Innards

OpenBSD lets you look at the internals settings of any UFS filesystem. I use this feature only rarely, most often when I can't understand why a program is behaving unexpectedly and I want to double-check everything I think I know.

The dumpfs(8) program is intended for debugging UFS internals, and provides intimate details on how the filesystem is arranged among cylinders and heads and other bogus geometry details. You can use it to check the characteristics of an existing unmounted filesystem. Give it one argument, the filesystem's device node. It produces pages of information, but the first five lines contain what I find most useful.

```
# dumpfs sd0a | head -5
magic    19540119 (FFS2) time    Wed Jul 20 17:56:54 2022
superblock location      65536   id      [ 61a5b3dc 76c17b04 ]
ncg      6         size    524288 blocks  504711
bsize    16384     shift   14      mask    0xffffc000
fsize    2048      shift   11      mask    0xfffff800
...
```

The first value is the *magic number*, identifying the type of filesystem. OpenBSD prints a handy reminder that yes, this number is assigned to FFS version 2.

You then get the date and time the filesystem was modified.

Further down, the *bsize* and *fsize* entries give the block and fragment size. Yes, this information appears in the disklabel, and newfs(8) uses the disklabel's values when creating filesystems, but when you're debugging a weird storage problem and want to be absolutely certain some clever idiot didn't override the defaults, verify the filesystem itself rather than look at what the filesystem is supposed to be.

The next dozen lines give the values of various filesystem internals. If you have an unhealthy degree of interest in filesystems, you can mostly decipher what they mean from fs(5). One that might catch your eye is *fsmnt*. This is the most recent location where this filesystem was mounted. I've relied on this value in situations too unpleasant to remember, mostly involving damaged systems.

The catch with dumpfs(8) is that it doesn't work on mounted filesystems. If you must investigate critical filesystems like /, you need to spend some time in single-user mode. The catch is, convenient programs like head(1) are not available in single-user mode. You can mount /tmp and save the output there, but OpenBSD purges /tmp at boot. That leaves you doing a dance like this.

```
# mount /tmp
# dumpfs sd0a > /tmp/sd0a.dumpfs
# mount -a
# mv /tmp/sd0a.dumpfs /root/
# exit
```

Investigating /tmp itself? Mount /home instead and put the output in your home directory.

If you go digging into the dumpfs(8) manual page, and from there into fsck_ffs(8), you'll find mentions of upgrading a filesystem. These upgrades are entirely within UFS1, and haven't been applicable for decades.[10] You can't upgrade a UFS1 filesystem to UFS2, you can only create a new filesystem.

---

[10]   Your patches to remove this code are eagerly awaited.

UFS Integrity

FFS is nothing but a meticulous ledger. Filesystem blocks go into certain disk sectors. Each file is written to specific blocks and fragments, all recorded in inodes. Every inode should be listed in directory records, and the whole thing should be glued together with superblocks. When you access a file, FFS looks up the location, finds the blocks, and presents the contents. It maintains a map of free blocks (the *free map*) and a list of inodes in use. When you remove a file, FFS purges all references to that file from its records. This ledger is no more complicated than it needs to be to keep track of millions of files. When you shut down an OpenBSD host the kernel completes all outstanding writes, unmounts it, and marks the filesystem as *clean*.

Everything works great, until you interrupt the record-keeping at the wrong instant. Perhaps a power failure as FFS is updating an inode, or a kernel panic as it's writing a new file to the disk. It's not that the data written to disk disappears, but the ledger telling FFS where to find the blocks is not internally consistent. Some inodes might contain records pointing to blocks that weren't written to yet, or refer to other inodes that don't exist. An inconsistent filesystem is called *dirty*. Filesystems mounted read-write are considered dirty, even if all outstanding writes have been completed. New data might arrive at any instant, after all.

At boot, OpenBSD automatically mounts all clean filesystems listed in `/etc/fstab`. If a filesystem isn't clean, it performs a minimal integrity check called *preening* that corrects minor problems like inodes that say they're in use but don't have any related files, or the free map listing blocks that files are using. Preening errs on the side of preserving data. If a preen can resolve every discovered error, the filesystem is marked clean and mounted and the boot continues.

If preening can't fix the filesystem, you have problems. Perhaps thousands of problems. You'll get messages much like this.

```
filesystem must be mounted read-only; you may need to
  run fsck
```

The system log shows messages more like this.

```
WARNING: R/W mount of /mnt denied.  Filesystem is not
  clean - run fsck
```

Your filesystem is messed up, and OpenBSD refuses to use it.

You have four options: use fsdb(8) and clri(8) to hand-stitch the filesystem back together, run fsck(8) manually, run fsck(8) automatically, or discard the filesystem and restore from backup. No matter what you choose, you can use dump(8) to preserve the dirty filesystem before changing anything. If you choose poorly and further corrupt the filesystem, you can revert to the less bad version.

Filesystem Debugging

You might know that filesystems are complicated, but the filesystem debugger fsdb(8) will teach you that they are even more complex than you thought. I don't want to discourage you from learning filesystem debugging, but you should prepare for it by spending some quantity time with the filesystem source code.

Do not attempt to learn the debugger during an outage. That will end poorly.

With the debugger fsdb(8) and the inode-clearing program clri(8), you can examine every error on the filesystem. You can connect blocks to their inodes, empty inodes that refer to blocks that are no longer used, and more. The catch is, you must already know what the data is supposed to look like; otherwise, you must work from lingering hints that might or might not be accurate. Repairing filesystems with the debugger is like stitching a damaged quilt back together by hand, if quilts had millions of pieces.

Running fsck(8) Manually

Maybe a dirty filesystem interrupted a boot and you're facing an unexpected single-user mode command prompt. Perhaps you plugged in a disk to check its contents, but you can't mount the dirty filesystems. Either way, you're facing fsck(8).

OpenBSD includes filesystem integrity checkers for FFS, FAT, and even Linux's EXT2FS. The fsck(8) program is a front end that redirects you to the correct integrity checker for the target filesystem. We'll focus on FFS. Run fsck(8) by giving it the device name of the filesystem you want to clean.

```
# fsck /dev/sd4d
```

Examining a large filesystem can take quite a while. Be patient.

The fsck program will find a number of different problems on a dirty filesystem: blocks that have lost their inodes, inodes that refer to empty blocks, and so on. Every problem must be resolved before the filesystem can be marked clean. The fsck program can often make a decent guess about how to fix each problem. When it finds one it can't fix, it asks you what you want to do.

```
...
** Phase 1 - Check Blocks and Sizes
** Phase 2 - Check Pathnames
UNALLOCATED  I=181914  OWNER=root MODE=40755
SIZE=512 MTIME=Jul 13 14:29 2022
DIR=/src/bin/ln

REMOVE? [Fyn?]y
```

Here's the directory for */src/bin/ln*. This filesystem is not mounted, so fsck considers the filesystem's uppermost directory to be the root. There's an incomplete directory entry, and fsck wants to remove it.

If you enter n, you are declaring that you will return with fsdb(8) and fix the problem yourself. If you enter y, you are approving this change. You will be prompted to approve every single change. The software wants to be absolutely certain that you understand that whatever it does is entirely your fault. If you accept every change, it will mark the filesystem as clean.

Sometimes, fsck(8) will find files but not be able to identify what directory they belong in. It puts these files in a */lost+found* directory in the filesystem root, with a temporary name. If a critical file is missing, you can use grep and strings to search for it.

Running fsck Automatically

Many sysadmins, myself included, have no choice but to trust fsck(8). I must accept that either `fsck` will either fix the errors or destroy the filesystem. If your filesystem was very busy, it might need hundreds or thousands of corrections. You could sit there for hours hitting y, y, y, all the while asking yourself "why? why? why?"

If you give `fsck` permission, it will do its best to fix every problem it can identify without any intervention from you. This is my go-to option. Use the `-y` option to tell `fsck` to run in automatic mode, changing everything in any way it sees fit. Every time it would normally prompt you, it assumes you said "yes."

```
# fsck -y /dev/sd4d
```

If you run `fsck` manually, but come to your senses partway through and realize you're going to hit y every time you're prompted, an F will switch to automatic mode.

If you're lucky, it repairs the filesystem and your files are intact. If you're not, it migrates some or all of your files into */lost+found.* you get to sort them out by hand. If you're very unlucky, you have a pristine but empty filesystem and must restore from backup. These changes were all done with your permission, though, so `fsck` has a clean conscience.

Space Usage

Filesystems fill up. That's what they're for. No matter how large you make your filesystem, eventually you're left wondering what's filling it up. OpenBSD has two primary tools for investigating disk usage, du(1) and df(1). The main problem with both of these is they haven't kept up with changing disk standards, and for good reason.

For decades, the standard disk sector size was 512 bytes. Sysadmins knew that one block was half a kilobyte, and could assess capacity by eye. As disks grew, sectors swelled, and filesystem block sizes expanded to cope. While OpenBSD UFS has a default block size of 8KB, that default is almost always overriden by values in the disklabel. Should du(1) and df(1) follow the disk sector size, or the filesystem block size?

Wrong question. Is it useful for them to do *either*? Nope. It isn't.

No matter the underlying block or sector size, these programs report everything in units of 512 bytes.

Before investigating anything about disk utilization, tell your environment to report everything in comfortable units using the $BLOCKSIZE environment variable. I used one-kilobyte blocks for many years but with current disk sizes, one-megabyte blocks are easier on the eye. I set $BLOCKSIZE to 1M for all my examples.

Space Per Filesystem and Reserved Space

Use df(1) to see how full each mounted filesystem is. The program displays the total number of blocks in the filesystem, the number of blocks used and available, as well as utilization as a percentage and the mount point.

```
$ df
Filesystem   1M-blocks        Used      Avail Capacity
Mounted on
/dev/sd0a          985         150        785     16%    /
/dev/sd0d         3962           0       3764      0%    /tmp
/dev/sd0e     67609690    67609036   -3379830    105%    /var
/dev/sd0f         5946        2505       3143     44%    /usr
...
```

The first entry, /dev/sd0a, has 985 one-megabyte blocks, or almost a gigabyte. 150 of those blocks are used, leaving 785 blocks available. It's only 16% full. Nothing to worry about here.

If you want to see a problem, check out the third entry—/dev/sd0e. It has 67,609,690 blocks, or roughly 64 GB. (Base two, remember?) Of those, it's used 67,609,036 blocks. Subtracting one from the other declares that we have a whopping 54 MB of free space. But df shows we have a negative number of blocks available and the filesystem is 105% full. What gives?

FFS needs an area of scratch space for moving files, defragmentation, and other maintenance tasks. By default, it's set

71

to five percent. When you exceed ninety-five-percent filesystem utilization, you eat into that scratch space. FFS switches from working as quickly as possible to cramming as many files onto the disk as compactly as possible. Performance plunges. Also, non-root users can no longer write files. This lets critical services continue to function so the sysadmin can log in and fix the problem.

It's entirely possible to change the amount of reservation with tunefs(8), but if you set it to below five percent FFS assumes it will never get a chance to clean up after itself and always focuses on efficient space usage. Disk performance can fall up to threefold. Leave it alone. If you want to temporarily stop non-root users from writing files, though, you can raise the reserved percentage above the current utilization. That's always amusing.

What's Filling Your Filesystem?

So the filesystem's overflowing. The question is, overflowing with what? Go into the filesystem and find the number of filesystem blocks used by each directory with du(1).

```
# cd /var
# du
2          ./audit
2          ./authpf
1330       ./backups
...
```

The output recursively lists every directory and subdirectory on the filesystem. You could eyeball the list, or you could be a sysadmin and let Unix do the work for you. Here I rank directories from smallest to largest.

```
# du | sort -nk 1
...
13806      ./db
67473922   ./mysql/vogonpoetry
67588686   ./mysql
...
```

Some databases deserve to be dropped.

If the full filesystem is the root filesystem, or another filesystem with other filesystems mounted beneath it, you might find the −x option helpful. It prevents du from leaving the current filesystem. If I know that my root filesystem is full, I don't want du to check the entire disk, only this filesystem.

```
# cd /
# du -h -d1 -x
2.0K     ./home
...
501M     ./dev
...
```

Uh oh. Looks like *someone* once again accidentally wrote to the non-existent device node for a disk, rather than a partition on that disk.

Human-Readable Output

Both du(1) and df(1) can provide "human-readable" output with the −h flag. This puts unit markers such as M and G in each column.

```
# df -h
Filesystem      Size     Used    Avail Capacity  Mounted on
/dev/sd0a       986M     151M     786M    16%    /
/dev/sd0d       3.9G    16.0K     3.7G     0%    /tmp
...
```

Human-readable output is fine for a quick look, but it obscures the relative size of each filesystem and makes sorting more difficult. Consider the *Size* column above. While 986 is larger than 3.9, 986 megabytes is not larger than 3.9 gigabytes. Using human-readable output isn't laziness, but don't let it make you lazy.

Adding New Disks

The installer guides you through partitioning your disks, but eventually you'll need to add storage to an existing system. Let's assemble what we've covered and add a new disk and filesystem to this host. We'll create a GPT, make a new filesystem, and use it to replace our overfull /var/mysql directory. I'll also set aside 1GB as an alternate root partition, as discussed at the end of this chapter.

73

Anytime you go near disks, partitioning, and filesystems, start by completely backing up your system. Tarballs, tarsnap, dump, whatever. Verify that backup before you touch your storage.

Partitions and Filesystems

OpenBSD found the new disk as `/dev/sd3`. It needs both a GPT and a disklabel. As always, make a plan before partitioning the disk. List each partition you need, and if it is a GPT or disklabel partition.

- an EFI boot partition (GPT)
- a 1 GB alternate root (disklabel)
- the rest for `/var/mysql` (disklabel)

From this list, work backwards. The GPT should include two partitions, one for the EFI and one for OpenBSD. The OpenBSD partition gets chopped in two, one for the alternate root and one for `/var/mysql`.

Creating the two GPT partitions is straight from Chapter 1.

```
# fdisk -A -b960 -y sd3
Writing GPT.
```

Verify the GPT looks correct before proceeding.

```
# fdisk sd3
Disk: sd3        Usable LBA: 34 to 1953525134 [1953525168 Sectors]
    #: type                           [       start:          size ]
---------------------------------------------------------------------
    0: EFI Sys                        [          64:           960 ]
    1: OpenBSD                        [        1024:    1953524111 ]
```

One EFI partition, one OpenBSD partition. That matches the plan. Now create a disklabel in the OpenBSD partition, assigning one partition for the alternate root and the other for the database data.

Now check the disklabel.

```
# disklabel sd3
...
#                size    offset   fstype [fsize bsize    cpg]
  c:        1953525168         0   unused
  i:               960        64    MSDOS
```

Partition *i* is the EFI space, and *c* represents the entire disk. Let's add a for the alternate root and d for data.

```
# disklabel -E sd3
Label editor (enter '?' for help at any prompt)
```

Add the *a* partition. For every prompt except the size, we just hit ENTER.

```
sd3> a
partition: [a]
offset: [1024]
size: [1953524111] 1g
FS type: [4.2BSD]
```

Now add the *d* partition. We want to use all the remaining space, so we can hit ENTER for every prompt except the partition letter.

```
sd3*> a
partition: [b] d
offset: [2104512]
size: [1951420623]
FS type: [4.2BSD]
```

Double-check your work, by printing the label in gigabyte units.

```
sd3*> p g
OpenBSD area: 1024-1953525135; size: 931.5G; free: 0.0G
#                size       offset  fstype [fsize bsize   cpg]
  a:             1.0G         1024  4.2BSD    2048 16384     1
  c:           931.5G            0  unused
  d:           930.5G      2104576  4.2BSD    8192 65536     1
  i:             0.0G           64  MSDOS
```

That looks good. Quit and save your work.

```
sd3*> q
Write new label?: [y] y
```

Once you exit disklabel(8), print the label again to verify your work. Then create your filesystem. An alternate root doesn't need a filesystem, but the database certainly does.

```
# newfs -q /dev/rsd3d
/dev/rsd3d: 952842.1MB in 1951420544 sectors of 512 bytes
292 cylinder groups of 3266.88MB, 52270 blocks, 104704 inodes
  each
```

We are now ready to move data to the partition.

Moving Partition Data

We're not just moving files from one partition to another. We are moving data from a partition to a replacement partition that will be mounted in the same place. I can't mount the new partition /dev/sd3d on /var/mysql and then copy files from the old /var/mysql to the new /var/mysql. Instead, I must mount the new filesystem at a temporary location, move the files from the original filesystem to the new filesystem, and mount the new filesystem at the desired location. That's exactly what /mnt is for.

```
# mount /dev/sd3d /mnt
```

This is temporary, so there's no need to use the DUID or make an /etc/fstab entry.

When moving files, use a program that preserves file flags such as tar(1), or dump(8) with restore(8). Here, I duplicate everything in /var/mysql in /mnt.

```
# tar -cf - -C /var/mysql . && tar xpf - -C /mnt )
```

You could add a -v somewhere in there to show progress, but filenames don't accurately represent progress when the files are all different sizes. Instead, use du(1) to see how many blocks are in the old directory and df(1) to watch the blocks in the new one increase.

The cp(1) and mv(1) programs do not guarantee to correctly copy file permissions and ownerships. I have never had trouble when using them, but in general programs like tar and cpio process file hierarchies most reliably. Only dump(8) and restore(8) can properly handle the file flags discussed in chflags(1), but OpenBSD does not encourage using file flags.

Editing /etc/fstab

When you've moved the data to the new filesystem, edit */etc/fstab* to make the new filesystem mount correctly at boot. We've used the device node for temporary mount, but always use a DUID in */etc/fstab*.

```
# disklabel sd3 | grep duid
duid: e80b3a6a2f6e66ef
```

Database files have no need for suid binaries or device nodes, so we can use an entry like this.

```
e80b3a6a2f6e66ef.d /var/mysql ffs rw,nodev,nosuid 1 2
```

Test the entry by mounting by filesystem name.

```
# umount /mnt
# mount /var/mysql
```

It should mount without complaint. The real test is if the system boots correctly. *Always* reboot-test filesystem changes!

With this, we've split */var* into two filesystems, */var* and */var/mysql*. We should have lots of space in */var*.

```
# df
Filesystem 1M-blocks      Used    Avail Capacity  Mounted on
...
/dev/sd0e       66025     66020    -3296     105%  /var
/dev/sd3d      945341     65872   832201      7%   /var/mysql
```

Wait—we moved files! How is */var* still overfull?

The tar(1) program does not move files. It duplicates them. We left the original files in place, and mounted */var/mysql* over them.

Filesystem Stacking

BSD filesystems are *stackable*, meaning you can mount one partition over another. The partition on top hides any files in the lower filesystem.

Suppose, purely hypothetically, that the contents of your /var/mysql directory have overflowed the entire /var filesystem, forcing you to add a new disk, create a new filesystem for /var/mysql, and move the database files there. Further suppose that you didn't actually move the files, but copied them instead.

When you start your database, it will read and write the files in your new /var/mysql filesystem. The old /var/mysql that's part of /var still exists. It's just hidden by having a filesystem mounted above it. It's not just that the space isn't freed up—if by any chance you should unmount the new /var/mysql, the database server will find old database files and act upon their contents. For any sort of commercial application or database-driven web site, this is disastrous.

Always remove data from beneath mount points. If you've already mounted the filesystem, unmount it, clean up, and remount it.

```
# umount /var/mysql
# cd /var/mysql/
# rm -rf *
# mount /var/mysql
```

We now have free space on /var, and no obsolete database files lurking to tempt disaster.[11]

Alternate Roots

You can screw up critical system files and grab intact copies from /var/backup. You can lose entire filesystems and still boot into single-user mode and recover data from the survivors. If you lose the root filesystem, however, there's no booting into single-user mode. You could install OpenBSD on a flash drive and boot from that. Or, you

---

[11]   If you're paranoid about globs you can run find /var/mysql -mindepth 1 -delete instead, but I live dangerously.

could use the *altroot* feature as an easy way to duplicate the root filesystem on a second disk.

If you enable altroot, OpenBSD duplicates your root filesystem on another partition every day during its `/etc/daily` cronjob. It's done via dd(1) rather than just copying files, so anything removed from your root filesystem is also removed from the alternate root. The alternate root must be on a different hard drive than the primary root. You can have only one alternate root, and the alternate root partition must be at least as large as the primary root.

An alternate root filesystem on a second disk gives you an easier path to recovery when the main disk fails. Use the system BIOS to boot the disk with the alternate root, and the host will come up using the previous day's configuration. Pulling data off the damaged system becomes a triage problem, rather than getting the host on the network and core services running.

Configure altroot in `/etc/fstab`. Give it a mount option of xx. In "Adding New Disks" previously this chapter, we created a 1GB `/dev/sd3a` for use as an alternate root. Disk `sd3` has a DUID of e80b3a6a2f6e66ef, so our `/etc/fstab` entry looks like this.

```
e80b3a6a2f6e66ef.a /altroot ffs xx 0 0
```

We identify the partition by DUID and letter, to avoid problems when drive numbers change. It has a mount point of `/altroot` and is of type ffs. The mount option is xx, however, which is not a valid option. It's your declaration that you know about this partition and want it overwritten every night. The 0 0 at the end tells the boot process to never check this filesystem for integrity.

You cannot mount `/altroot` from this `/etc/fstab` entry. You could mount it by device node at the command line if you need to verify its contents.

Now that it's configured, enable it by adding ROOTBACKUP=1 to `/etc/daily.local`.

Growing Filesystems

You add disks to free up space on your existing disks. Sometimes that disk isn't partitioned the way you want, however. If you combine everything we've learned, and are lucky, you can change that without reinstalling. You'll also need basic math, like subtracting large numbers and correctly multiplying seven by nine.

The growfs(8) program lets you expand a filesystem, but it's trickier than it sounds. A filesystem can only be expanded into empty space immediately after the existing filesystem. If you have an empty partition at the beginning of the disk, but want to grow a filesystem at the end of the disk, you're out of luck and all you can do is say, "oh no not again." But let's see how this works.

The trick to growing a filesystem is that a filesystem is just a bunch of bits on a partition. OpenBSD partitions are just chalk lines between sectors. When you create a filesystem, it grows until it hits the line and stop. By erasing some of those lines, you create a larger partition. You use growfs(8) to tell the filesystem "hey, you have more room."

One of my hosts has a 1.6GB /usr/local partition. When I installed the host, I thought it was big enough. I was wrong. Let's see what might be done. Partitions are defined in the disklabel, so let's look.

```
...
#         size       offset   fstype [fsize bsize   cpg]
...
g:     1118240      9041472   4.2BSD  2048 16384  8666 # /usr/X11R6
h:     3756224     10159712   4.2BSD  2048 16384 12960 # /usr/local
i:         960           64   MSDOS
j:     3293184     13915936   4.2BSD  2048 16384 12960 # /usr/src
k:    10928160     17209120   4.2BSD  2048 16384 12960 # /usr/obj
l:     5415520     28137280   4.2BSD  2048 16384 12960 # /home
```

Partition *h* is /usr/local. It is immediately followed by partition *i*, the EFI boot partition. You can manipulate disks in many ways, but eliminating the boot loader is frequently counterproductive. But look more closely. Partitions are shown in *letter* order, not *block* order. All those horrid size and offset numbers tell the real story. Partition *i* begins on sector 64 and has an offset of 64 sectors. The only thing in front of it is the actual GUID partition table.

Partition *h* has a size of 3756224 sectors and an offset of 10159712. The partition that really follows it will have an offset of (3,756,224 + 10,159,712 =) 13,915,936. That's the offset of partition *j*, or /usr/src. Adding the size and offset of partition *j* gives us (3,293,184 + 13,915,936 =) 17,209,120, the beginning of partition *k* or /usr/obj.

I perfectly well understand why OpenBSD creates these partitions. It's faster to newfs(8) /usr/obj than recursively delete files, and adding the partitions after install is impossible. But this host uses binary updates via sysupgrade(8), and I have many copies of the OpenBSD source tree at hand. These partitions can go away.

Before editing filesystems or partitions on a live system, perform a complete backup. Schedule the work for a time that you could perform a complete reinstall and restore. A basic math error can wreck the system.

We could do this in single-user mode, but I believe I'm an advanced life form and see no reason to bother. We do need to put the machine in a maintenance mode, shutting down any web servers or databases or other applications, leaving only the services you need to access the host.

Unmount the partitions we're going to remove and the partition we will expand.

```
# umount /usr/local
# umount /usr/obj/
# umount /usr/src
```

With these partitions unmounted, we can edit the disklabel. My drive is sd2. Create a backup label first.

```
# disklabel sd2 > sd2.label
# disklabel -E sd2
```

Begin by removing /usr/src and /usr/obj, or partitions *j* and *k*, using the disklabel editor's d command.

```
sd2> d
partition to delete: [] k
sd2*> d
partition to delete: [] j
```

Stop and check your work. Print the modified disklabel.

```
sd2*> p
OpenBSD area: 1024-33552814; size: 33551790; free: 14221378
#           size       offset  fstype [fsize bsize   cpg]
...
  g:     1118240      9041472  4.2BSD  2048 16384  8666 # /usr/X11R6
  h:     3756224     10159712  4.2BSD  2048 16384 12960 # /usr/local
  i:         960           64  MSDOS
  l:     5415520     28137280  4.2BSD  2048 16384 12960 # /home
```

Figure out the size of the new filesystem. You could add up the sizes of each partition you deleted, or simply subtract the offset of partition *h* from the offset of the next partition, *l*. The new size is $(28137280 - 10159712 =)$ 17,977,568.

Now modify partition *h* to have the new size, using the disklabel editor's m command.

```
sd2*> m h
offset: [10159712]
size: [3756224] 17977568
FS type: [4.2BSD]
```

That should be okay. The interactive disklabel editor stops you from creating overlapping partitions, so the worst you could do is leave empty space. Inspect your work again.

```
sd2*> p
OpenBSD area: 1024-33552814; size: 33551790; free: 34
#           size       offset  fstype [fsize bsize   cpg]
...
  g:     1118240      9041472  4.2BSD  2048 16384  8666 # /usr/X11R6
  h:    17977568     10159712  4.2BSD  2048 16384 12960 # /usr/local
  i:         960           64  MSDOS
  l:     5415520     28137280  4.2BSD  2048 16384 12960 # /home
```

This looks sane. Double-checking on my calculator shows that 17,977,568 should fill the gap between 10,179,712 and 28,137,280. Commit the change.

```
sd2*> w
sd2> q
```

The disk has a new label. You have changed the partitions. Even now, the change is not irrevocable. The old /usr/src and /usr/obj filesystems are still on the disk. Only the lines between them have been erased. We could always restore the label from the backup you took. If you ignored my advice and didn't take a backup, you'll find backup disklabels in /var/backups.

Now we check to see what growfs(8) would do if you expanded sd0h, by using the -N flag.

```
# growfs -N /dev/rsd2h
new filesystem size is: 4494392 frags
Warning: 144608 sector(s) cannot be allocated.
```

All this work, and some sectors can't be added to the filesystem? More math shows that this is about 70KB. New filesystems lose these tiny slices all the time. You wouldn't even notice if we weren't desperate for space. Move on.

```
growfs: 8707.5MB (17832960 sectors) block size 16384,
fragment size 2048
  using 43 cylinder groups of 202.50MB, 12960 blks, 25920
  inodes.
super-block backups (for fsck -b #) at:
  4147360, 4562080, 4976800, 5391520, 5806240, 6220960,
  ...
```

This looks much like newfs(8), as it should. If growfs saw any problems, it would declare them.

At this point, my old filesystems are still on the disk. I could restore the old disklabel and walk away. I need the space, so I overwrite them.

```
# growfs /dev/rsd2h
We strongly recommend you to make a backup before
  growing the Filesystem

 Did you backup your data (Yes/No) ? Yes
```

You could skip this warning with the −y flag, but this is your last chance to back out. Check your backup. If you're confident, type Yes with a capital Y. You'll see the usual newfs(8) block allocation, and your filesystem has grown.

Grown filesystems must be cleaned before you can mount them.

```
# fsck -y /dev/rsd2h
```

You can now mount your new filesystem.

You aren't done, though. Remove the deleted partitions from /etc/fstab, or the next boot will hang trying to mount them. Perform a reboot test just to be certain you didn't screw up. At the end, though, we have a lovely 7.8GB /usr/local.

Understanding FFS and disk partitioning gives you the core of OpenBSD storage administration. Everything else is details. Unfortunately, there are a *lot* of those details...

OpenBSD scores over the older, more pedestrian BSD in two important respects. First, it can be freely downloaded, rather than distributed on tape. Second, it has a blowfish as a mascot.

—Hitchhiker's Guide to OpenBSD

Chapter 3: Memory, Swap, and the Buffer Cache

If stashing filesystems on disk isn't enough for you, you can put filesystems in memory and memory on disk. No, you can't put filesystems on disk in memory on the disk because one—that would be silly, and two—that's what the buffer cache is for.

What's the buffer cache, I hear you ask? Oh dear. We'd better start there.

The Buffer Cache

Some files on disk get read more often than others, or get repeatedly read for a short time and are then abandoned. Suppose you're in a terminal session, browsing around the filesystem tree looking for a certain file that you know you stuffed in some directory. You'll make heavy use of commands like file(1) and ls(1), and possibly strings(1) and grep(1) and a few other favorites. If your shell had to read each of these commands from disk every time you ran them, performance would plunge.

The *buffer cache* is a portion of system memory dedicated to keeping copies of the most recently used files. When you read a file from disk, the kernel retains a copy in the buffer cache. If the file is needed again, and the version on disk hasn't changed, the file gets served from the cache rather than disk. OpenBSD reserves about 20% of the system's memory for the buffer cache, although it's not always fully utilized, especially on modern systems. Check top(1) for an easy view of the current buffer cache size.

85

The kernel maintains the list of files retained in the buffer cache, starting with the most recently used. Each time you read a file, it's put on top of the list. When the buffer cache exhausts its allocated memory and you read a new file, it discards items from the bottom of the list until there's space for the new file. This isn't perfect—some silly person is going to decide they need that file immediately after it's been discarded—but on the average it's a smart bet.

Other caching systems exist, but OpenBSD doesn't use them.

Should you tune the size of the buffer cache? Probably not. The actual cache is almost always smaller than what's allowed, but you need headroom for surges of activity. If the buffer cache is consistently hovering right around 20% of RAM *and* your disk activity is always high, and you have enough free RAM, you might consider increasing the sysctl `kern.bufcachepercent`. Watch the system for any instability, however, or for memory pressure. Increasing the buffer cache size and making the host swap is counterproductive.

Swapping, I hear you ask? Okay, let's talk swap.

Swap Space

When you installed OpenBSD, you allocated a partition for "swap space." Swap space serves as really slow memory. When the host runs low on physical memory, it can shove objects that it must retain in memory but haven't been used for a while onto the disk. When those objects are needed, the kernel reads them from disk. Basically, swap space transforms disk I/O and space into extraordinarily inefficient RAM.

Moving bits and pieces of programs into swap is called *paging*. Paging isn't necessarily bad—the old saying that programs spend 80% of their time running 20% of their code is a cliché because it's so often true. Initialization, error handling, and shutdown code get called less often than the code that does… whatever the program is about. *Swapping* is when the host is so short on memory that it scoops up whatever programs aren't running this microsecond and shoves the entire thing onto disk. Swapping is bad, but it's better than the system crashing.

Now that even laptops ship with 64GB RAM, do you need swap? Yes, you do, for two reasons. One, never underestimate a random program's ability to gobble memory. Two, if you discover an OpenBSD bug and panic your system, the kernel dump will get written to your swap partition. If you want the option to debug kernel panics, you need a swap partition slightly larger than your physical RAM.

Swap is a vital component of virtual memory. A host's *virtual memory* is the total amount of memory it can address, including physical RAM and swap space. A host with 64 GB or RAM and 64GB of swap has 128GB of virtual memory. When the kernel allocates memory to a program, it hands out a piece of virtual memory. The kernel works behind the scenes to decide if that memory is in RAM or in swap. Programs can request memory that can't be written to swap, but the kernel decides if it will condescend to grant such requests—or not.

The catch with such large virtual memory is that programs can slowly nibble it up. Hardware platforms like amd64 support allocating a single program multiple terabytes of memory. If a host has that 128GB of virtual memory, a program with a slow memory leak could eventually nibble it all up, causing creeping performance degradation.[12] OpenBSD's resource limits (set in `/etc/login.conf`) should throttle such behavior, but misconfigurations happen.

Viewing Swap

Look at your host's swap configuration with swapctl(8).

```
# swapctl
Device       1M-blocks  Used  Avail  Capacity  Priority
/dev/sd0b        32292     0  32292        0%         0
```

This host is using disk partition *sd0b* as a wap space. It's about 32GB, and completely unused.

---

[12]   Hopefully, you would notice a program that *quickly* devoured 128GB of memory.

The filesystems listed in swapctl should match the contents of /etc/fstab, but you do have the option of mucking with it. On this host, hot-swappable drives *sd0* and *sd1* each have 64GB swap.

```
# swapctl
Device         1M-blocks   Used   Avail Capacity  Priority
/dev/sd0b         66615       0   66615        0%         0
/dev/sd1b         66615       0   66615        0%         0
Total            133230       0   98908        0%
```

I need to replace drive *sd1*. If you yank a drive with an active swap partition, the kernel will throw a wobbler. Tell the kernel to stop using partition *sd1b* as swap with swapctl's −d flag, then remove the drive.

```
# swapctl -d /dev/sd1b
```

No output. Did it work?

```
# swapctl
Device         1M-blocks   Used   Avail  Capacity  Priority
/dev/sd0b         66615       0   66615        0%         0
```

The kernel is no longer using that drive. You can unmount the other partitions and remove the drive. Once you've replaced and repartitioned the drive, slip *sd1b* back into the swap pool with the −a flag.

```
# swapctl -a /dev/sd1b
```

OpenBSD supports swap features that probably shouldn't be used, such as assigning priorities to different swap partitions and paging over NFS. If by some malignant chance you find yourself in a place with modern hardware where swap over NFS seems prudent, consider instead adding memory to your system or dividing the workload between hosts.

Swap Encryption

Swap space is special in that it contains memory structures. A savvy intruder that examines non-sensitive information written to swap can learn a lot about the host's role and the organization it supports. This information remains on the disk until overwritten, persisting even after a reboot. These characteristics make swap space snooping a realistic threat.

Running programs can contain sensitive data such as passwords, SSH authentication keys, private keys for encryption, and more. Programs that use such material should request memory that will never be paged, but if a struggling host swaps out an entire program sensitive information can be written out.

OpenBSD encrypts swap by default. New encryption keys are generated at every boot. While those data structures remain on the disk after a reboot, the kernel no longer has the keys to read it.

Memory Filesystems

A computer can use a filesystem on any backing store that can hold data. Before hard drives, we used punch cards, magnetic tape, and even punched tape. System memory holds data until you turn off the computer, so it can also back a filesystem. A *memory filesystem* (MFS) or *memory disk* lives in the host's RAM. Reading and writing files to and from a memory filesystem is much faster than accessing those same files on a spinning disk. They are only a marginal improvement over SSDs, but if you have sufficient memory they still make sense for certain applications.

Don't implement MFS before you understand its limitations. Memory doesn't persist after system shutdown or a kernel panic, so a reboot will erase the filesystem. Unlike destroying a disk-backed filesystem, you can't use filesystem debugging tools like fsdb(8) to dig up the contents. They are literally *gone*.

You can use an MFS partition to rapidly process short-lived files. Building packages on an MFS can make sense, provided you're not trying to compile something large like OpenOffice. Many people like having a speedy, ephemeral /tmp, but SSDs have made that less of a concern and OpenBSD clears /tmp at boot anyway.

Some database-driven applications need fast storage for dozens or hundreds of fast-changing short-lived lock files. I would certainly consider using MFS in such a role.

MFS works even when the system uses a small amount of its swap space. The kernel retains any information being actively used in RAM, while transferring less-frequently accessed memory onto disk-backed swap. Swap-backed MFS is no worse than writing to disk. It is an added complication, though, so if you want to use MFS be sure to have lots of memory. If you run short on virtual memory, replace your MFS with an SSD-backed filesystem and see what happens.

You might encounter references to an "efficient" memory filesystem, tmpfs. It's included in OpenBSD, but as of 7.2 does not work. Everything except the man page is disconnected from the build. Do not let the presence of mount_tmpfs(8) confuse you.

Creating MFS Filesystems

Use mount_mfs(8) to create memory filesystems. OpenBSD's mount commands require two arguments, a physical device and a mount point. Memory filesystems don't have a device node, so use a swap space device node instead. If you have multiple swap partitions, any of them will work. Specify the memory filesystem's size with the -s flag. Here I create a one-gigabyte memory-backed filesystem on /mnt.

```
# mount_mfs -s1g /dev/rsd0b /mnt
```

If you request a larger memory filesystem than your system can support, you'll get the warning `mmap: Cannot allocate memory. Set a smaller size.` The maximum size of a MFS varies with your hardware architecture.

If you run mount(8) you'll see the MFS, but you might notice that it's mounted asynchronously. Mount options that help ensure filesystem integrity after an unexpected shutdown make no sense for an ephemeral filesystem. Soft updates aren't supported, because—why?

Asynchronous writes are perfectly safe for something you're going to throw away.

Mounting MFS at Boot

Use `/etc/fstab` to create a shiny new MFS at boot. You need only a mount point and partition size.

```
swap /mnt mfs rw,async,nodev,nosuid,-s1g 0 0
```

You don't need to specify a specific swap device—OpenBSD will grab one. Just as with any other partition, you must specify the mount point and the filesystem type. Very few temporary filesystems need device nodes or setuid programs, so disable them. Do not leave a space between the `-s` and the size of the MFS, because `/etc/fstab` uses white space as field separators. Set the last two values to zero. A MFS never needs fsck(8), and if you're backing up an ephemeral filesystem your system design has gone spectacularly wrong.

Now let's dive into how OpenBSD supports foreign filesystems.

"Meanwhile, the poor Unix command line, by effectively
removing all barriers to communication between differ-
ent programs and systems, has caused more and bloodier
flame wars than anything else in the history of creation."

—Hitchhiker's Guide to OpenBSD

Chapter 4: Foreign Filesystems

While OpenBSD is designed to use the Fast File System, it also has
limited support for filesystems used by other operating systems.
Some of these, like the ISO9660 filesystem used on CDs and the UDF
filesystem found on DVDs work very reliably. Others, like Linux and
Microsoft Windows filesystems, are more useful for extracting data
from old disks.

OpenBSD supports foreign filesystems either through in-kernel
features and a specific mount(8) command, or via add-on programs
and the Filesystem in Userspace (FUSE) interface and third-party
packages. OpenBSD might not have complete access to all the
filesystem's features, and not all filesystems work well with OpenBSD's
features. Unix's file permissions and ownership model do not map
neatly onto NTFS' permissions scheme, and the venerable FAT lacks
any concept of ownership. Plan your use of foreign filesystems within
their limits.

One of those limits is that these filesystems don't have inodes.

Inodes and Vnodes

OpenBSD (and most other Unix variants) expect to address
filesystems via inodes. When the kernel wants to see what blocks
are in a file or which files are in a directory, it consults inodes. This
practice runs inextricably throughout the kernel, and replacing or
supplementing it for every new filesystem would be intrusive and
destabilizing. The FAT filesystem doesn't use inodes, Linux's EXT

filesystem uses inodes that are incompatible with FFS, CDs do something entirely different, and the UDF format found on DVDs bear little resemblance to either. These filesystems all have some sort of index, though, so BSD uses an abstraction layer to convert them into digestible inodes.

The *virtual node*, or *vnode*, is a synthetic inode. You will never directly manipulate vnodes but documentation, bug reports, and developers refer to them constantly. Every filesystem read or write passes through a vnode. When you write to an FFS filesystem, the kernel addresses the data to a vnode, which is mapped to an inode, which maps the file on disk. When you write to a FAT filesystem, the kernel addresses the data to a vnode exactly like before. OpenBSD's support for the filesystem, whether in the kernel or in userspace, has a table for mapping vnode characteristics onto the filesystem-specific qualities.

Do you need to know how to manipulate vnodes? Nope. You do need to understand that vnodes belong to OpenBSD and not the filesystem, though, so you won't go looking for why a mount_ntfs(8) bug mentions vnodes when the Microsoft documentation doesn't.

Integrated Foreign Filesystems

OpenBSD includes support for FAT, ISO9660, UDF, EXT2 and 3, and early NTFS, but not all of these are recommended for production use. We'll look at each.

FAT

The FAT (File Allocation Table) filesystem became popular on early Microsoft operating systems and is still very common on digital cameras and non-optical removable media like flash drives and floppy disks. These days, it's considered the minimum viable filesystem and is available on almost everything. OpenBSD has built-in support for all major versions from the last few decades, including FAT12, FAT16, and FAT32, and manages them with mount_msdos(8).

I copied an MP3 album from a Windows box onto a flash drive and stuck the drive into my OpenBSD machine, where it's recognized as *sd4*. How do I get at the files? While OpenBSD assigns letter *i* for FAT partitions outside the OpenBSD physical partition, verify that with disklabel(8).

```
# disklabel sd4
...
16 partitions:
#             size offset  fstype [fsize bsize    cpg]
  c:       4162560      0  unused
  i:       4160771     64  MSDOS
```

As expected, partition *sd4i* is the FAT filesystem. Mount it.

```
# mount /dev/sd4i /mnt/
```

Wait—that's plain mount(8). What about mount_msdos(8)? The mount(8) command recognizes many different filesystems, and calls the appropriate version of mount to handle the lowly grunt work. Use umount(8) to disconnect it, same as any other filesystem.

ISO9660

The ISO9660 filesystem used on optical media like CDs and DVDs, and is intended for permanent data storage. Optical drives show up as */dev/cd* devices, no matter how they connect to the host. The filesystem itself is usually on the *a* partition, but sometimes gets dumped straight on *c*.

Use mount_cd9660(8) program to manage these disks, but you can call it from plain old mount(8).

```
# mount /dev/cd0a /mnt
```

Unmount with umount(8), as always.

If you're interested in making ISO9660 images to burn to disk, consider mkhybrid(8) and cdio(1). Optical media, especially the read-write variety, is a poor long-term data storage option. Some disks endure, but a good percentage of them decay. Plus, the maximum size of an ISO9660 filesystem is 4.3 GB, which is almost nothing today.

UDF

Universal Data Format (UDF) is the replacement for ISO9660, but more flexible and with support for larger disks, like DVDs and Blu-Ray. OpenBSD can mount and read UDF-formatted disks with mount_udf(8).

Support for UDF does not mean support for reading commercial Blu-Ray disks or DVDs. Film studios encrypt their disks specifically so you can't mount and copy them like a normal disk. You can't even read the disklabel. There is no freely available legal solution for watching movies on disk on OpenBSD, or any open-source operating system.[13]

If you have an unencrypted UDF disk, however, mount_udf(8) will mount it. The UDF is normally on partition *a*.

```
# mount /dev/cd0a /mnt
```

Many optical disks use a hybrid format where software recognizes them as both ISO9660 and UDF. Use whatever you can bludgeon the operating system into recognizing.

OpenBSD's mkisofs(8) can create UDF images for burning to disk.

EXT

The Extended Filesystem (EXT) is the most commonly used Linux filesystem. OpenBSD can reliably read EXT2 and EXT3 using mount_ext2fs(8). It can also read EXT4 filesystems that use 128-bit inodes, which means it can't read most modern EXT4 filesystems unless they're specifically formatted to be compatible with OpenBSD. The simplest way to discover if OpenBSD can read a disk is to check the disklabel to identify partitions, and try to mount them.

Linux is a Unix workalike, and builds many of the same features on similar concepts. Linux programs do not run on OpenBSD, so the setuid binaries should be harmless. Most Linux versions use a device filesystem rather than on-disk device nodes, so an EXT filesystem shouldn't have device nodes.

---

[13]   Search engines can provide a number of solutions that read commercial DVDs perfectly fine, except for the "legal" part.

The phrase "this shouldn't ever happen" means "if it ever happens it will be super bad, so take extra precautions against it." Always mount EXT filesystems with `nodev` and `nosuid`.

```
# mount -o nodev,nosuid,noexec /dev/sd4j /mnt/
```

The tricky thing about using EXT filesystems is file ownership. Both FFS and EXT identify users by user ID number (UID). A cursory comparison of `/etc/passwd` between OpenBSD and any Linux system will show the similarity between the two is zero.[14]

If you have trouble mounting a modern EXT filesystem on OpenBSD, consider transferring data using either using NFS or tar(1).

NTFS

OpenBSD integrates read-only support for NTFS filesystems, as used by modern Microsoft operating systems. In my experience, NTFS is the one filesystem where OpenBSD's mount(8) might have difficulty identifying the correct way to mount it. Check the disklabel to identify partitions, and use mount_ntfs(8) to mount. Files on NTFS often show up as executables, so I defend against mayhem by mounting it `noexec`. I also assume Microsoft will cleverly betray me and add other defensive options.

```
# mount_ntfs -o nodev,nosuid,noexec /dev/sd4i /mnt/
```

This read-only support lets you extract files from NTFS disks, but if you want to write data to NTFS filesystems, consider the FUSE NTFS implementation discussed later this chapter.

Foreign Filesystem Ownership

Filesystems like FAT and ISO9660 have no concept of file ownership and permissions, while NTFS' ownership scheme is incompatible with OpenBSD's. When you mount any of these filesystems, the files are owned by `root:wheel` and inherit the permissions of the mount point. This might be too restrictive for your application. Linux's EXT filesystems have a Unix-compatible permissions scheme, but the

---

[14]   UID zero, `root`, is the same on both, so it's zero similarity.

file owners and groups are almost certainly incompatible with your OpenBSD host.

Work around these problems by assigning an OpenBSD account and group to own the mounted files. Specify the owner with -u, and a group with -g.

Here's how root would mount that same NTFS filesystem, but have everything owned by my account.

```
# mount_ntfs -o nodev,nosuid,noexec -u mwl \
  -g mwl /dev/sd4i /mnt/
```

When giving an unprivileged user ownership of a filesystem, protections like noexec, nosuid, and nodev are especially vital.

Filesystems in Userspace

Filesystems in Userspace, or FUSE, is an interface that allows userland programs to present vnode devices to the kernel. This lets people develop userland programs to predigest the messy intricacies of filesystems.

Why would anyone do this? Filesystems are messy, and actual files written on disk are messier. If you make a mess of the kernel, the operating system panics. In system administration, *DON'T PANIC* is not something that should be printed everywhere in large, friendly letters; it's a prayer. Isolating filesystem-related mayhem from the kernel is worthwhile. Also, kernel programming differs from userland programming. The differences can be learned and practiced, but if a risky thing can be done outside the kernel, why not leave it there? Finally, the ability to call userland programs from a filesystem makes a whole bunch of weird things possible. OpenBSD will never integrate an SSH client into the kernel, but with FUSE you can mount directories on other hosts using SSH as a transport. FUSE programs frequently require only minor changes to work on multiple operating systems.

FUSE is not perfect. Both FUSE and the kernel sanitize data, but a bizarrely corrupt or deliberately malignant filesystem might slither through those sanity checks. A clever intruder might be able to exploit that. FUSE is less efficient than kernel-based filesystems, but it allows data transformations that would be difficult or impossible in the kernel.

While other operating systems might allow unprivileged users to mount filesystems, OpenBSD is resolute that only `root` gets to bulldoze the directory tree. Some FUSE modules might require extra configuration to work as you might expect—while your account might be able to connect to the SSH server you want to access just fine, can `root`?

As of OpenBSD 7.2, OpenBSD has packaged five FUSE modules. With fuse-zip you can mount zip files read-only. The exfat-fuse module gives access to the exFAT filesystem used on embedded systems. While OpenBSD removed unionfs for being notoriously buggy, unionfs-fuse lets you combine multiple filesystems into one. The ntfs-module lets you not only read NTFS filesystems, but write to them. I'll illustrate OpenBSD's FUSE with the overwhelmingly popular sshfs-fuse (aka SSHFS), which lets you mount filesystems over SSH.

sshfs-fuse

Install sshfs-fuse from packages. It's tiny, as it relies on the various SSH programs.

You must be able to log into the target server, from the local `root` account to a remote unprivileged account. You need shell access to the destination server, and access to the desired directory. Never allow logins as `root`. If this SSHFS will be used by multiple people, you should create a new unprivileged account that can access the desired directory. If it's just for your personal convenience, say from your workstation to a server, use your own account. I strongly recommend key-based authentication. You might need to create a new key for SSHFS, or to allow your SSH agent's environment variables to survive doas(1). If any of this confuses you, permit me to recommend my book *SSH Mastery* (Tilted Windmill Press, 2018).

Once your SSH client works, invoke sshfs(1) to mount the remote filesystem. At a minimum you need the remote server username, the hostname, and the local mount point.

sshfs *user@server: /local-directory*

The colon after the hostname is mandatory. Here, I'm logged in as `root`. I mount the home directory of user `mwl` on the server `www` on `/mnt`.

sshfs mwl@www: /mnt

The contents of my home directory on the remote server are now available in `/mnt`. I can edit and copy files as much as my permissions permit.

To mount a different directory on the SSH server, put it after the colon.

sshfs mwl@www:/var/www /mnt

Change the port by adding the –p flag.

sshfs -p 2222 mwl@www: /mnt

You can add other SSH options with –o, exactly as with ssh(1), or use –F to point at a configuration file.

FUSE Permissions

By default, only the user who mounted the FUSE filesystem can access it. Don't do routine work as `root`, however. Additionally, FUSE maps file ownerships by UID. Without distributed authentication, users probably have different UIDs on each system. Neither FUSE nor sshfs do anything to coordinate user information.

Allow other users to access this mount point with sshfs' `allow_other` option.

sshfs -o allow_other mwl@www: /mnt

While unprivileged users can now go into this directory, the file ownerships are probably totally scrambled. The UIDs of file owners and groups are unchanged from the remote system, but they are

interpreted as per the local host's standards. You can assign the files
in an sshfs mount to be owned by a specific user by using the `idmap`
option. You must specify a user and a group to map remote files onto.
Here, I declare that local user and group 1000 own all the files in the
sshfs.

```
# sshfs -o idmap=user,uid=1000,gid=1000,allow_other \
  -p 822 mwl@www: /mnt
```

This works well when you're mounting a remote user's home
directory, where you can realistically expect all the files to be owned
by the user connecting to the host. If you mount a different directory,
such as /tmp or your web site directory, the local system will still show
those permissions—but the remote server will enforce permissions as
it understands them.

You can also create a file mapping local and remote UIDs
and groups, but at that point you're probably better off installing
centralized authentication.

Other FUSE filesystems have restrictions imposed by the transport
medium or the format. You can't write into the middle of ZIP files, so
fuse_zip is read-only. You can't reformat an NTFS as FFS via FUSE,
because you're addressing filesystem blocks and the raw disk. But the
basics of using FUSE itself are fairly similar between plugins.

With this, let's look at mounting filesystem images.

Mounting Filesystem Images

OpenBSD's *vnd* device provides a layer of vnodes. By attaching a file
to a *vnd* device, you insert vnodes between the file and the kernel,
allowing the kernel to treat the file as a disk. This *vnode device* lets
you access the contents of a disk image without any tedious mucking
about with real hardware. You can use the regular mount commands to
access the filesystem's contents. When you're finished, detach the image
from the device node and you can manipulate the image as a file.

Use vnconfig(8) to attach files to a vnd device. Just as with a
physical disk, the image might have MBR or GPT partitions, a
disklabel, or be a naked filesystem.

Vnode Devices

The default kernel has four vnode devices. If you must simultaneously mount more than four disk images, edit your kernel binary to increase the number. You'll also need to create the device nodes in /dev.

Take a look at /dev/vnd0. You'll see it has sub-devices vnd0a, vnd0b, and so on, just like any other disk. You'll also see raw devices, such as /dev/rvnd0 and /dev/rvnd0a. Always use the c partition in vnconfig commands; if the image has recognizable partitions, OpenBSD will assign other partition letters as needed.

Attaching Vnode Devices to Disk Images

When attaching a vnode device to a file, the vnconfig(8) command needs two arguments: the desired device node and the file name.

```
# vnconfig vndX filename.img
```

A while back I had to recover privileged passwords from a whole stack of Windows machines, and copy a file to each system. The free Trinity Rescue Kit would let me reset the passwords. It's distributed as an ISO. The easiest way to get the file on each system would be to put it on the password recovery media. TRK can be installed on a FAT16 flash drive, if you copy files from the ISO. Everything starts with mounting the disk image. ISOs are entire disks, so they use the c partition. Here I attach /dev/vnd0c to the disk image, and mount the resulting vnode device.

```
# vnconfig vnd0c trinity-rescue-kit.3.4-build-372.iso
# mount /dev/vnd0c /mnt
```

I can now extract the files to a flash drive, copy my new file to it, and fix all these machines.

Managing Vnode Devices

Vnode devices attached to a file stay that way until deliberately disconnected. Each vnode device can be attached to only one file at a time. If you're not sure which devices are in use, use vnconfig -l.

```
# vnconfig -l
vnd0: covering trinity-rescue-kit.3.4-build-372.iso on
    sd0l, inode 10601493
vnd1: covering ufs.img on sd0l, inode 10601492
vnd2: not in use
vnd3: not in use
```

The list shows the vnode device with the backing file, and then the partition and inode of that file. My TRK image is on partition *sd0l*, and the file has the inode 10601493. I also have the file *ufs.img* mounted, on partition *sd0l*, and my specific file uses inode 10601492.

Let's take a look at *vnd1*. I have no memory of mounting this.

```
# disklabel vnd1
# /dev/rvnd1c:
type: vnd
disk: vnd device
label: fictitious
duid: 525e1dc0ebc09a8a
flags:
bytes/sector: 512
sectors/track: 100
tracks/cylinder: 1
sectors/cylinder: 100
cylinders: 2048
total sectors: 204800
boundstart: 1024
boundend: 204767
drivedata: 0

16 partitions:
#           size        offset  fstype [fsize bsize    cpg]
  a:        03712         1024  4.2BSD    2048 16384   1577
  c:        04800            0  unused
  i:          960           64  MSDOS
```

This looks like an image of a complete disk? A quick check shows that I can mount */dev/vnd1a* and */dev/vnd1i*. Running fdisk vnd1c reveals that this disk has two physical partitions, one EFI and one OpenBSD. I can manipulate this image just like a real disk.

OpenBSD has no protections against moving, altering, or destroying the underlying file while it's attached to a vnode device.

If I remove the image file, that specific vnode remains in the configuration. More than once, one of my flunkies deleted a file backing a vnode device and desperately created a file with the same name. The vnconfig program provides filenames as a friendly convenience, but like all other programs uses inodes internally.

```
# ls -i ufs.img
10601494 ufs.img
```

The inodes don't match, so the vnode is not attached to this file. Use find(1) to search out files by inode and conclusively demonstrate that the flunky did not recover from his screwup.[15]

Detaching Vnode Devices

Vnode devices remain attached to a file until specifically disconnected, and each vnode device can be attached to only one file at a time. Disconnect vnode devices that are not in use with the -u flag to vnconfig. If I'm done with the filesystems on *vnd1*, I would run:

```
# vnconfig -u vnd1
```

I can now use this vnode device elsewhere.

Removable Media

While floppy disks have faded into niche uses, and even optical drives are less common, removable media like external hard drives and flash drives have proliferated. While you can't be absolutely certain that any random flash drive will have a single partition *i* and be formatted in some species of FAT, and not every CD has a single ISO9660 filesystem covering the entire disk, these are certainly the most common. Make life easier on your OpenBSD workstation by creating */etc/fstab* entries for them, like so.

```
/dev/cd0c /cdrom cd9660  ro,noauto,noexec,nosuid,nodev
/dev/sd4i /flash msdos   rw,noauto,noexec,nosuid,nodev
```

---

[15]   Having flunkies is not fun—except some of the shouting I quite like.

Now you can mount a CD with `mount /cdrom` or a flash drive with `mount /flash`. You'll need to create these directories. Be sure to use separate directories for different devices—remember, BSD has stackable mounts, and you don't want the contents of one device hiding the others. This leaves */mnt* free for other media, NFS, or whatever else you dredge up.

You can make an entry for a vnode-backed device to mount an image easily with two */etc/fstab* entries. The first attaches the disk images to a vnd device. Note that the filesystem type is *vnd*. That instructs mount(8) to call mount_vnd(8) to handle this filesystem.

```
/var/images/ufs.img /dev/vnd0c vnd rw 0 0
```

The second mounts the vnd device, just like any other mount point.

```
/dev/vnd0c /mnt ffs rw,nodev,noexec,nosuid 0 0
```

When you want to use the filesystem image, mount the vnd device and then the mount point.

```
# mount /dev/vnd0c
# mount /mnt/
```

Automatically mounting a FUSE varies wildly with the type of filesystem, and is not possible for certain varieties. Check each FUSE module's documentation for details.

You can now handle most non-native filesystems easily. Let's consider accessing filesystems over the network.

"This is obviously some strange usage of the word 'secure'
that I wasn't previously aware of."

— Hitchhikers Guide to OpenBSD

Chapter 5: Network File System

The *Network File System*, or *NFS*, allows a host to mount filesystems on another host. NFS originated in UNIX, but most modern operating systems support some version of it. OpenBSD has complete support for NFS versions 2 and 3. NFS is a complicated protocol with a tangled history, so we won't discuss the intricacies of the protocol or large-scale deployments. This chapter will help you integrate OpenBSD into a complicated NFS environment, but you'll need additional resources to create that environment.

The best way to learn NFS is to set up two virtual machines. One will be your test NFS server, the other the client. Make sure that your account has the same UID and GID on both hosts. Install both of these on a LAN shielded from the public Internet by a packet filter or other isolating mechanism and follow along with the examples in this chapter.

NFS Essentials

NFS is a client/server protocol documented in a plethora of RFCs. The NFS server offers filesystems to other computers. Filesystems on offer are called *exports*. NFS clients can mount those exports in almost the same way they mount local filesystems. Network communication is performed by Sun RPC, so the server must run the portmap(8) service. RPC connections might use TCP and/or UDP ports 1024 through 5000, and daemons related to NFS use other scattered ports, so many firewall administrators object to passing it on general principle. Some NFS implementations allow you to restrict which ports everything uses, but OpenBSD is not among them.

NFS is stateless. The NFS server does not track the condition of each connection. When you reboot a server, the client does not receive an error. The client can't access the network filesystem, but the NFS protocol itself doesn't declare "oops, that server isn't there any more, disconnecting." Once the server returns, the filesystem transparently reappears. Yes, applications and users might well notice the missing filesystem, but NFS itself doesn't. Extensions and enhancements such as rpc.statd(8) add stateful elements to NFS. Statelessness also means that proper file locking isn't possible. Most implementations use add-on programs like rpc.lockd(8) to provide file locking. OpenBSD supports file locking as an NFS server, but not as a client.

NFS identifies file ownership by UID and GID. If your account on the client has UID and GID 1000, and the server exports files owned by UID and GID 1000, you own those files. If you have consistent UIDs and GIDs across your environment, such as from a distributed authentication system, file ownership will be consistent. If each host has basically random UIDs based on whose account was created first, you'll have to do some trickery to map user IDs between machines. The nobody user was specifically created to cope with NFS ownership issues.

OpenBSD is known for security and encryption. NFS is not. Access control is by IP address, UID, and GID. None of these are encrypted. Neither is the protocol. Anyone with a conveniently located packet sniffer can view every transaction, and those with the proper expertise can even understand them. Never use NFS on or across the open Internet, only on a protected network.

The NFS protocol has evolved since Sun made it public in 1984, and many of those variations have been implemented by nearly every operating system. Other BSDs, Sun-derived systems, Linux, Apple, and Microsoft operating systems can interoperate with OpenBSD's NFS, but different versions and environments might require occasional tweaks. If you have problems, study mount_nfs(8) for entire lists of things to try. If your answer isn't there, feed the details into your favorite search engine. It's almost certain someone already had your problem.

If you have trouble with NFS, check `/var/log/messages` for errors. If you've repeatedly reconfigured your NFS server because you're learning how things work and things stop working, reboot your NFS server and client. Starting with a clean stack solves many problems. Once you understand how all the pieces fit together, though, NFS changes should never require a reboot.

The NFS Client

OpenBSD's NFS client works without any preliminary configuration. If you want to mount a filesystem from an NFS server, start by checking that the server's RPC is available to this client. Use rpcinfo(1) and the -p flag with the server hostname to probe the host. Here I check and see if the host `towel` supports NFS.

```
$ rpcinfo -p towel
program vers proto    port
 100000   2    tcp     111   portmapper
 100000   2    udp     111   portmapper
 100005   1    udp     779   mountd
...
 100003   2    udp    2049   nfs
...
 100021   0    udp     624   nlockmgr
...
 100024   1    udp     879   statusb
 100024   1    tcp     608   status
```

You'll get a list of all the RPC services available to your host. The server `towel` runs the RPC services *portmapper*, *mountd*, and *nfs*, so it's offering basic NFS file sharing. The *nlockmgr* service is part of rpc.lockd(8), so it also supports file locking over NFS. OpenBSD clients don't support those locks so we don't care. The *status* service is rpc.statd(8), which helps the server but not us so again, we don't care.

If the server offers NFS, check and see what it exports with showmount(8).

```
# showmount -e towel
Exports list on towel:
/home        Everyone
```

Any host can mount this server's /home, so let's do that. You could run mount_nfs(8), but mount(8) works as well for routine use.

```
# mount hostname:export mountpoint
```

Here I try to mount /home residing on the host **towel** on the client's /mnt.

```
# mount towel:/home /mnt
```

If it returns silently, the server and client negotiated NFS connection settings and you have a new NFS mount. If not, that filesystem is not shared with you. Go configure the server to export it.

Client Options

NFS clients and servers negotiate their protocol settings. Sometimes those negotiations fail. Sometimes the results are sub-optimal, or the connection keeps collapsing because the Minimum Viable NAS isn't viable. What can you do?

Stop negotiating. Make demands. The mount_nfs(8) command lets you fine-tune the connection settings. Most of these are not useful for the average case, but can be invaluable when a mount misbehaves.

NFSv3 can use both TCP and UDP. OpenBSD prefers UDP, but TCP is generally more effective on high-bandwidth or high-latency networks. Force use of TCP with -T.

```
# mount_nfs -T towel:/home /mnt
```

Sometimes an NFS connection is unstable because both sides claim to support NFSv3, but their implementations aren't exactly interoperable. Fall back to a slower but perhaps more reliable NFSv2 mount with the -2 option.

When all else fails, read mount_nfs(8). Many of the options are useful only in bizarre environments, but you might find solutions there.

Broken Mounts

One advantage of NFS is that it's stateless. One disadvantage of NFS is that it's stateless. When a server stops responding, the client has no way to know if it's because of a network failure, server reboot, or because the server has been hurtled to the end of the universe and will never return. That doesn't matter for a protocol like HTTP, which has built-in timeouts and error codes and stuff, but NFS is an eternal optimist that believes that it can complete all outstanding reads and writes if it just waits long enough. It will wait forever.

Patience is commendable, but from the user's perspective, they type ls and the command hangs forever. They can't interrupt it. They can't CTRL-C out of it. The only escape is killing the terminal window and starting over. If you're on the console, too bad. I want the option to break hung mounts. I want NFS to try for a couple minutes, then come back and say "Nope, sorry." You can configure NFS to be less tolerant in two ways: *soft* mounts and *interruptible* mounts.

A *soft* mount tries each filesystem request up to ten times, waiting ten seconds for each, then quits. Enable soft mounts with -s, or with the *soft* mount option. Change the number of retries with -x.

An *interruptible* mount will try forever, but programs hung up because of failed NFS access will acknowledge a CTRL-C and give you your terminal back. Enable interruptible mounts with -i, or the *intr* mount option.

Almost all of my NFS clients use both. Soft, interruptible mounts are the best way to cope with NFS.

NFS and /etc/fstab

You can list an NFS mount in */etc/fstab*, for automatic or easy manual mounting. The catch is that any delay in automatic mounting of an NFS export will delay the boot. If the NFS server is unavailable for any reason, the client won't finish booting. If the host reboots during a DNS failure, the boot will hang. Making automatic NFS mounts soft and interruptible, and listing them by server IP address rather than hostname, are vital for resilience.

Here's an `fstab` entry for a NFS mount.

```
203.0.113.48:/home /data nfs nodev,rw,nosuid,soft,intr 0 0
```

The server is given as an IP address and export. The mount point is shown exactly like any other mount point. The filesystem type is *nfs*, and the options that follow should look familiar. The 0 0 at the end tells the host to neither `fsck` nor `dump` the NFS mount.

Most filesystems are mounted early in the boot process, but NFS exports can't be mounted until after the network is started. Test your boot process repeatedly to verify that the NFS filesystem mounts correctly, that programs requiring that mount start correctly, and that you haven't introduced unexpected circular dependencies.

NFS Versions

NFSv1 was Sun's internal development version. When Sun opened the protocol, they bumped the version number to 2 so the whole world could unwittingly help them test their backward compatibility features.

NFS version 2 was very simple. It uses only UDP and was meant for low-loss local networks. It is not generally recommended today, but if you have a client and a server that absolutely refuse to interoperate, try kicking the connection back to NFSv2 and see what happens.

NFSv3 is an incremental improvement over NFSv2. It supports using TCP, making it more usable on high-bandwidth or high-latency connections. Extensions like rpc.lockd(8) and rpc.statd(8) offer a semblance of state. Many of NFSv2's sharp edges that didn't work so well in reality have been smoothed over.

Rather than another incremental improvement, NFSv4 is an entirely new protocol designed to accommodate high-capacity file services. It is much larger, stateful, and includes features such as Windows-compatible[16] Access Control Lists. NFSv4 is complicated in exactly the way OpenBSD isn't, so developer interest in implementing

---

[16]   Nearly compatible. Very nearly compatible. Compatible in every single way except the one most important to you, I'm sure.

it is very low. NFS versions 2 and 3 do suffer from the Year 2038 problem, however, so this area is ripe for your well-tested patches.

The NFS Server

OpenBSD's NFS server requires three daemons: mountd(8), nfsd(8), and portmap(8). The `mountd` daemon processes the export configuration, decrees whether or not client mount requests can be met, and gives out file handles for mounted filesystems. The `nfsd` daemon listens for incoming NFS I/O requests and routes them into the kernel. The `portmap` daemon listens for incoming NFS RPC requests and steers them to whatever port `mountd` and `nfsd` are listening on. The rpc.lockd(8) and rpc.statd(8) daemons are also helpful. Lockd provides file locking services to clients that support it. Statd monitors connections, so that when a client disappears the server can release resources dedicated to that client. Enable everything with rcctl(8).

```
# rcctl enable portmap mountd nfsd lockd statd
```

You must have an *exports* file, with at least a newline in it, before the NFS-related daemons will start correctly.

Exporting Filesystems

Define which clients may mount which filesystems and/or directories in */etc/exports*. This file takes a single line for each unique combination of disk partition and clients. Each line has up to three parts:

exported-directories export-options clients

Only the exported directory is mandatory. The directory path cannot contain symlinks or dots. If I wanted to export the */home* partition read-write and invite every single host on the Internet to bulldoze it, I could use this *exports*.

```
/home
```

Any time you edit /etc/exports, you must tell mountd(8) to reread it. If you're following along with these examples to learn NFS, reboot the server after configuring this first export. Otherwise, you can merely reload mount(8).

```
# rcctl reload mountd
mountd(ok)
```

Your client should now be able to mount the filesystem. Have your client mount the server's /home and see if you can run touch test in any directory with suitable permissions.

Clients can mount only the exact directory listed in /etc/exports. Suppose I'm interested in only the contents of my home directory, /home/mwl. It would make sense for me to mount /home/mwl rather than the entirety of /home. The server explicitly exports /home, however. That's the only directory I can mount.

Read-Only Mounts

If you want to be slightly less welcoming to the entire Internet, you can export a filesystem read-only. Use the -ro option in the *exports* entry.

```
/home -ro
```

Reload mountd(8), and all clients with existing mounts are immediately unable to write files. The statelessness of NFS means that the server only notifies clients that the mounts are now read-only when they attempt to alter the filesystem. Conditions can change between individual writes.

Select Directories

We often need to export only subdirectories of a filesystem. To export multiple directories in the same filesystem, list them both in /etc/exports separated by a space.

```
/home/fprefect /home/apdent -ro
```

Clients may mount the directories /home/fprefect and /home/apdent, but other directories like /home/tmcmillan are invisible to clients. You can list any number of directories on the same line, so

114

long as they are all in the same filesystem.

To export multiple directories from different filesystems, list them on separate lines.

```
/home
/var/mysql -ro
```

Sometimes you want to let clients mount any directory within a filesystem. The /home filesystem is a great example. A shell server might have dozens or hundreds of users, and any one of them might want to mount their home directory across the network. Give the mount point and the -alldirs option to give clients that flexibility.

```
/home -alldirs
```

The -alldirs option only works when exporting an entire mount point. If it doesn't show up in the server's df output, you can't use -alldirs on it.

Over on the client, I can now unmount /home and mount only my home directory.

```
# umount /mnt
# mount towel:/home/mwl /mnt
```

I now have my files, without having to wander through other people's irrelevant cruft. Or, if someone's irrelevant cruft suddenly becomes relevant, I can mount their home directory and grab it.

Mapping Users

NFSv3 provides no username information between client and server, so file ownership and permissions are managed entirely by UID. If your usernames and UIDs are synchronized across all your systems, whether by LDAP or rdist(1) or an intern with a shell script, things work transparently—until someone misbehaves. You can configure your NFS servers to treat remote users with different levels of privilege than their UID would normally offer. We'll consider root, then regular users.

root And NFS

Everybody has `root` access on their workstation. Even if the workstation is locked down by a corporate sysadmin who's not actively evil but merely bad tempered, bureaucratic, officious, and callous, the user has physical access to the device. They can get `root`. An NFS server cannot trust client machines with the ability to write files as `root`. Uploading arbitrary binaries to the main fileserver never ends well, and a breach of one client would mean a breach of the whole network.

By default, NFS requests from UID and GID 0 are mapped to UID -2. With 16-bit IDs, this becomes 32767. OpenBSD assigns this to the user and group `nobody`, specifically created for and dedicated to NFS.[17] When `root` on a client tries to read a directory or write a file, the server performs the task as `nobody`.

Use the `-maproot` option to direct `root` accesses to a user other than `nobody`. If I created a special account `nfsroot` to handle requests from `root`, I would configure it as so.

```
/var/log -maproot=nfsroot
```

Group permissions are a powerful but often overlooked access control. Give any groups that the remote root account is considered a member of after the username, separating everything by colons. Here, my syslog server exports its logs so that clients can use their own CPU to process them. Clients running as root access this export as `nfsroot`, with membership in `logread` and `webmasters`.

```
/var/log -maproot=nfsroot:logread:webmasters
```

With root maps, I don't need to add the `nfsroot` account to any groups on the server. I can assign wholly different group memberships to different exports.

---

[17] On lesser operating systems, you will occasionally encounter programs configured to run as `nobody`. Whoever configured them should be thrown out an airlock.

```
/var/log -maproot=nfsroot:logread:webmasters
/home    -maproot=nfsroot:helpdesk
```

Does the group `helpdesk` need access to the logs? Who cares, bypass the whole problem.

User Mapping

If you can't trust a client's UIDs and GIDs, what can you trust?

Not a dang thing. That's why you can forget trusting users and map all user accesses on an export to a single account, using the `-mapall` option. Perhaps you have an export where permissions don't really matter, such as a document repository or a set of read-only data. You can remove permission issues by declaring that all NFS requests will be treated as a single user.

```
/docs -mapall=nfsuser
```

You can add group memberships after the username by separating them with colons, exactly as with mapping a root account.

```
/docs -mapall=nfsuser:customers:helpdesk
```

Precise control of user access helps protect your NFS server.

Permitted NFS Clients

If you don't declare a list of clients permitted to access the export, NFS permits all hosts access. This is sub-optimal. You can restrict the clients permitted to access your NFS server by listing their IP address at the end of the *exports* entry.

```
/home 203.0.113.9
```

Giving access to an entire subnet is the preferred way to grant access to many hosts. NFS predates widespread use of the familiar slash notation (203.0.113.0/24) and requires you use the options `-network` and `-mask` to specify a subnet.

```
/home -network=203.0.113.0 -mask=255.255.255.0
```

You can also use hostnames, but they make NFS vulnerable to DNS failures so I pretend they're not an option.

Putting everything together, here's how you would restrict NFS access to one host and make it read-only.

```
/var/log -ro 192.0.2.99
```

Even if you're behind a NAT or very strong packet filter, I strongly encourage you to develop the good habit of listing permitted clients in */etc/exports*.

Multiple Exports on One Filesystem

You can have only one line for each combination filesystem and permitted clients. If */home* is a single filesystem, this is an illegal *exports* file.

```
/home/fprefect -maproot=nfsroot 203.0.113.99
/home/apdent 203.0.113.99
```

Two directories on the same filesystem exported to the same host? No. And */var/log/messages* will tell you so.

What you *can* do is export directories on one filesystem to different hosts with different permissions.

```
/home/fprefect -maproot=nfsroot 203.0.113.99
/home/apdent -ro 203.0.113.100
```

You win a game of */etc/exports* by figuring out how to combine hosts, directories, filesystems, and permissions such that you achieve the desired access.

You can now use NFS to access remote filesystems. Let's bypass filesystems and seize entire disks over the network.

"No, that's just perfectly normal paranoia.
Every sysadmin has that."

—*Hitchhikers Guide to OpenBSD*

Chapter 6: iSCSI

Accessing block devices through iSCSI is a terrible way to expand system capacity. A network is much slower than the local bus. A cheap modern SATA connector gives each port six gigabytes a second, enough to saturate forty-eight gigabit links. For iSCSI to be reasonably effective, you need to establish a private storage network with top-end network cards and a switch that can actually handle the traffic the marketing department claims. It's quite dreadful.

Sometimes, "quite dreadful" is your best choice.

The Small Computer System Interface (SCSI) interface has become the industry standard for storage devices. Actual SCSI devices vanished from new hardware decades ago, but the SCSI commands survive in modern SAS and SATA drives. iSCSI tunnels SCSI commands inside a TCP connection, letting a host issue storage commands to another host over a media not intended for block storage. But at least it's faster than 20th-century ATA-5 drive.[18]

iSCSI is a client-server protocol disguised as traditional SCSI. It uses SCSI terminology rather than network terminology, but once you understand the words it's a straightforward client-server application. The client, or *initiator*, initiates all iSCSI activity. The server, or *target*, accepts those requests and performs I/O. It's no different than any other storage device. OpenBSD supports iSCSI initiation via iscsid(8).

An iSCSI *portal* is the IP address and TCP port where iSCSI targets listen to the network. iSCSI routinely listens on TCP port 3260, although that's not mandatory. A *portal group* is a group of portals on multiple IP addresses.

---

[18]   Barely.

Like NFS, iSCSI is not intended for use on the public Internet. Always protect your iSCSI servers with a restrictive packet filter or other network isolation. Unlike NFS, it presents raw block storage to the client. You can newfs(8) an iSCSI device, fsck(8) it, even swapon(8) it if you want a laugh.

OpenBSD has integrated basic support for connecting to iSCSI devices as a client. It can also be an iSCSI server with add-on software, but that's not OpenBSD's strength and we won't discuss it. The implementation doesn't support CHAP authentication or have fancy discovery tools. But you can attach disks, read and write on them, and cleanly detach them during system shutdown. If networked disk seems like a sensible solution, it will suffice.

iSCSI Device Naming

Both initiators and targets use an iSCSI-specific naming scheme that can bewilder newcomers. OpenBSD initiator names aren't as horrid—you can almost pretend that `iqn.1995-11.org.openbsd.iscsid:towel` means something. Why would anyone name a disk `iqn.1996-03.com.sun:01:1a7d978ca…` that trails off into a meaningless hexadecimal string like someone trying to down three pints of bitter in ten minutes? It's not quite so confusing once you understand what you're looking at. Each name is made up of distinct components separated by periods.

Device names are *iSCSI Qualified Names* (*IQN*), indicating a specific drive shared by a specific organization. They declare this by starting with `iqn`. IQNs start with the most general information possible, and become more specific as they go on. Not all IQNs include all pieces.

After `iqn` there's the month and year the organization creating the name was established, separated by a dash. What does "established" mean? Some organizations use the date they were founded, or the date they started using iSCSI, or the date the storage admin gave up.

The organization's domain name follows, in reverse order. Why reverse order? It's likely that `detroit.mwl.io` and `paris.mwl.io` have entirely different organizations managing their disks, and the IQN must reflect this.

The software supporting the iSCSI device comes next.

Last, you have a name for this specific device. Target names indicate a SCSI array, perhaps including several disks or only one. Initiators often contain the hostname.

Consider a default OpenBSD initiator name, `iqn.1995-11.org.openbsd.iscsid:towel`. It starts with `iqn`, fine. The `1995-11` means that the managing organization considered itself established in November 1995. It's followed by `org.openbsd`, so this device is managed by OpenBSD. It connects using `iscsid`. After the colon we get a hostname, `towel`. This is the initiator on the host **towel**, which runs OpenBSD. No problem.

Target names might be less obvious, but if you control them you can make them less painful. Take `iqn.2013-11.io.mwl:towelDisks`. This is an IQN for an organization founded in November 2013, **mwl.io**. I could argue that this domain name represents me and I was established over fifty years ago, but some programmer somewhere didn't expect mid-twentieth-century years in the IQN so I'm being practical. I named this target after the host it's provided for, adding the qualifier *disks* to make its role obvious.

The names are almost identical. The only difference is one is `towelDisks` and the other, `towel`. IQNs must be unique within an organization, and you do want to know which name is the host and which the disks. Work with iSCSI enough and you too will learn to skip most of the IQN and see only the important stuff at the end.[19]

If names can be this specific, why do vendors provide us those long hexadecimal strings? They're trying to provide globally unique defaults for all their users, so they use some variant of GUID. Take control of your IQNs. The names are private, and nobody outside your organization will ever see them. Use meaningful names. If your domain name is long, abbreviate it.

---

[19]   Until everything breaks, at least.

Configuring iSCSI

Configure iscsid(8) in `/etc/iscsi.conf`. Here's a complete configuration for a single target.

```
target1="iscsi.mwl.io"
myaddress="203.0.113.48"

target "nas1" {
  initiatoraddr $myaddress
  initiatorname iqn.2013-11.io.mwl:towelHost
  targetaddr $target1
  targetname iqn.2013-11.io.mwl:towelDisks
}
```

This should look highly familiar to anyone who has ever configured any service on OpenBSD.

You can use macros in `iscsi.conf`, exactly as in many other OpenBSD configuration files like `pf.conf`. Macros make sense when a value might change. I define two macros here, `target1` and `myaddress`. The target uses a hostname, because the storage administrator insists I do so. OpenBSD's `iscsid` insists on knowing a specific source address to connect from, and I want to be able to easily move this machine without changing entries for multiple iSCSI targets.

We then have the first target, `nas1`, with four keywords.

Use `initiatoraddr` to tell `iscsid` the source IP address of all iscsid(8) connections. I set this to a macro.

The `initiatorname` is an IQN you configured for this target. If you don't configure one, OpenBSD will use its default.

With `targetaddr` and `targetname`, you tell `iscsid` the IP address of the iSCSI target and the IQN of that target.

Configuring iSCSI within an organization requires an exchange of information with your storage administrator. Figure out your client's IQN and its IP address. If the host has multiple IP addresses, figure out which it will use to connect to the target. Configure them in `iscsi.conf`. Your storage administrator will want all of these when they give you the target address and name. If the storage administrator offers you any variety of CHAP authentication, OpenBSD can't use it. They must disable CHAP before OpenBSD can connect. In a large organization with strict policies, this administrative issue is often the biggest problem in using OpenBSD's iSCSI.

Using iscsid(8)

Once you have a working configuration, enable and start iscsid.

```
# rcctl enable iscsid
# rcctl start iscsid
```

If you did everything correctly, you should see new disks appear in */var/log/messages* and the hw.disknames sysctl.

If no new block devices appear, however, iscsid(8) is not very good at telling you why. I find the easiest way to debug problems is with a packet sniffer. There is an iscsid control program, iscsictl(8), but it gives very little debugging detail. It does provide statistics on how much you're utilizing your iSCSI devices, however, when you run iscsictl show vscsi stats.

Changing Configuration

Targets change, NASes offer new targets, and sometimes you need to disconnect disks. OpenBSD doesn't have a graceful method for reconfiguring iscsi targets. To change the configuration, start by unmounting the disks. This lets the kernel complete any outstanding writes. You can't use rcctl to stop the iscsid process; you must pkill iscsid to detach the drives.

Why is iscsid hard to kill? When a host shuts down, storage is supposed to persist until the very end so the kernel can complete the final writes and mark the filesystems clean. The kernel has specific code to prevent it from terminating iscsid with the rest of the daemons at shutdown.

If you want a whole bunch of disks, it's best to have them locally. Like in the next chapter.

"Files are an illusion. Filesystems doubly so."

—*Hitchhiker's Guide to OpenBSD*

Chapter 7: Redundancy

Storage media fails. Spinning disks lock up, SSDs scramble, optical media decays, stone tablets crumble. Computers are supposed to be above failure, and folks have tried to make every system redundant on every level. Redundant Array of Independent Disks (RAID) technology is how we work around failing storage media, allowing computers to continue to serve data even as the underlying hardware staggers and dies. If a drive fails, the system can continue to run without data loss until you replace the failed drive—or until a second drive fails. RAID can be provided by hardware or software.

Hardware RAID seems nice. You plug in a card, attach the drives to the card, work through a handy menu, and poof! Redundancy! A hardware RAID card is a disk controller that runs its own operating system. The controller achieves redundancy by distributing reads and writes between the attached disks. Hardware RAID is really software RAID, provided by black box software. The catch is that these RAID controllers are not generally interchangeable. One RAID-5 controller usually can't read disks managed by a different RAID controller. If the controller dies, you must replace it with the exact same model of controller. It's probably obsolete, so you'll go to the pricey secondhand market or restore from backup onto a new but equally non-interoperable RAID controller. It's enough to make the most mild-manner sysadmin reconfigure the computer with a very large axe.

If you run your RAID in the operating system, you have to manage the operating system. But the disk format will remain interoperable. If your disk controller fails, you toss in a new controller and carry on.

You don't risk having to restore from backup because of proprietary hardware. While hardware RAID might look easier at installation time, in the long run software RAID is more maintainable.

OpenBSD has solid support for software raid in its softraid(4) framework. The bioctl(8) RAID management program can manage softraid devices as well as many hardware RAID controllers. Between the two, you can support the common RAID types without an expensive hardware controller. In this chapter, we'll set up several sorts of software RAID with softraid(4).

Softraid Disciplines

Softraid's support for a storage transformation, including RAID, is called a *discipline*. Softraid disciplines cannot be combined; you can't stack RAID-0 on RAID-1 to create RAID-10. You could stack OpenBSD's software RAID on top of hardware RAID, but that's rather missing the point. Control everything through the softraid management device node `/dev/softraid0`.

Softraid uses partitions, not disks. Each partition has a filesystem type of *RAID*. A partition dedicated to softraid is called a *chunk*. The softraid virtual disk is called a *volume*. You can use partitions of different sizes, but each softraid chunk will use an amount of space equal to the smallest partition. If you mirror a 5TB partition and a 10TB partition, each chunk will be only 5TB. While no two 1TB disks from different manufacturers are truly the same size, avoid wasting capacity and try to use disks that are at least *marketed* as similar sizes.

Here are commonly used unencrypted softraid disciplines.

RAID-0: Striping

This combines multiple disks into a single larger virtual disk. You can glue two 10TB drives together to create a single 20TB virtual disk. It has zero redundancy, however. Loss of any one physical disk means complete loss of the virtual disk. RAID-0 is faster than a single disk or any other RAID discipline. It's most useful for when you need large, fast, disposable storage, such as in many big mathematical modeling systems.

You can't boot from RAID-0 softraid.

On the command line, use the option *0* to indicate RAID-0.

Concat

A concatenated softraid is much like RAID-0, but it can use partitions of different sizes. If you want to combine a 1TB and 5TB disk into a single storage entity, concatenation lets you do that. It has all the vulnerabilities of RAID-0, and all the lopsided performance you'd expect.

You can't boot from concatenated softraid.

On the command line, use a lower-case *c* to indicate the concat discipline.

RAID-1: Mirroring

The contents of one disk are duplicated on another. The host scatters reads between the two disks, but duplicates all writes. The size of a mirror equals the smallest drive in the array. If one drive fails the data remains intact and the system continues running. Presumably, your monitoring system will let you know about the failed drive so you can replace it.

You can boot from mirrored disks.

On the command line, use the option *1* to indicate RAID-1.

RAID-5: Striping With Parity

The current industry standard for redundancy, RAID-5 includes redundancy data. A RAID-5 array needs at least three disks, but the loss of any one disk does not lose any data. Read and write requests are scattered between the disks, improving throughput. The size of the RAID-5 array is the size of the smallest disk in the array, times one less than the number of disks in the array. If a RAID-5 has five 10TB disks, the array will have a capacity of 10x(5-1)=40TB.

You can't boot from a softraid RAID-5.

On the command line, use a *5* to indicate RAID-5.

Softraid Partitions

Each softraid chunk is a disk partition. You have to create the partitions beforehand. I'll assume you're using GPT partitioning on fairly modern hardware. Claim an entire disk in the name of OpenBSD with fdisk's -g flag.

```
$ fdisk -gy sd5
Writing GPT.
```

Repeat this for every disk.

Now label your disks. Before creating the first label, however, check the size of each disk with fdisk. Look for the number of sectors on the disk, at the end of the first line.

```
# fdisk sd5 | grep Sectors
Disk: sd5     Usable LBA: 34 to 1953525134 [1953525168 Sectors]
```

This disk has 1,953,525,168 sectors. Repeat this check for every softraid disk. When creating your softraid disklabel, always start with the smallest disk first. This time, disk *sd5* is the smallest. Create a single disklabel partition covering the entire disk.

```
# disklabel -E sd5
Label editor (enter '?' for help at any prompt)
sd5> a
partition: [a]
offset: [64]
size: [2097055]
FS type: [4.2BSD] raid
sd5*> w
sd5> q
```

This disk is now labeled for softraid.

The disklabel editor isn't bad, but rather than walk through it for all of my devices I'm going to grab the label for *sd5* and apply it to all of my disks. Disklabel will retain each disk's different DUID, but the partitioning will be identical.

```
# disklabel sd5 > disklabel.sd5.softraid
# disklabel -R sd6 disklabel.sd5.softraid
# disklabel -R sd7 disklabel.sd5.softraid
# disklabel -R sd8 disklabel.sd5.softraid
# disklabel -R sd9 disklabel.sd5.softraid
```

All five disks are now identically labeled, with partition *a* dedicated to softraid.

The disks themselves are not identical, however. Why not use any leftover space on each disk? It is entirely possible to make a softraid volume containing a 2TB disk and a 3TB disk, and make a conventional partition out of the larger drive's excess space. It seems optimal, right?

RAID is about resilience, not efficiency. In optimizing disk space utilization, you're also optimizing for slowness and failure. The two drives probably have similar I/O capacity, and are probably connected to the same controller. Accessing that "optimized" partition will degrade that disk's softraid performance, and slow down the entire softraid device. Also, a disk that is more heavily used that its peers is more likely to fail.

Initializing Softraid Volumes

Initialize new softraid volumes with bioctl(8). Use -c to specify a discipline. Give the included partitions with -l. At the end, the softraid management device node *softraid0*.

```
# bioctl -c discipline -l partition1,partition2... \
  softraid0
```

This host has several disks available for softraid, *sd5* through *sd9*. Suppose I want to combine *sd5a* and *sd6a* into a mirrored (RAID-1) volume.

```
# bioctl -c 1 -l sd5a,sd6a softraid0
softraid0: RAID 1 volume attached as sd10
```

Our new volume attached as */dev/sd10*. You'll probably need to create a device node for it.

```
# sh MAKEDEV sd10
```

Any random junk at the beginning of the volume might confuse the kernel, so wipe out the new volume's first megabyte. If you've previously wiped out the disk, you can skip this.

```
# dd if=/dev/zero bs=1m count=1 of=/dev/sd10c
```

Give the softraid volume a GPT, a label, and a filesystem.

```
# fdisk -gy sd10
# disklabel -E sd10
Label editor (enter '?' for help at any prompt)
sd10> a
partition: [a]
offset: [64]
size: [10482463000]
FS type: [4.2BSD]
sd10*> w
sd10> q
# newfs sd10a
```

Our new volume is ready to use.

The more disks you have, the better the chance that a disk will get a different device name at boot. Always use the softraid device's DUID when you create `/etc/fstab` entries,.

Managing Softraid

The whole point of RAID is to recover from failure, which means you must know when devices fail. Use bioctl(8) to view the state of a softraid device. If you know the device node for the volume you can use it, or you can ask `softraid0` to dump all the volumes it knows about.

```
# bioctl softraid0
Volume       Status            Size Device
softraid0 0 Online     17179549184 sd10      RAID1
          0 Online     17179549184 0:0.0     noencl <sd5a>
          1 Online     17179549184 0:1.0     noencl <sd6a>
```

Both disks are online and available.

Suppose some jerk reaches into the computer and rips out one of the drives. What happens?

130

```
# bioctl softraid0
Volume        Status              Size Device
softraid0 0 Degraded    17179549184 sd10       RAID1
          0 Online      17179549184 0:0.0      noencl <sd5a>
          1 Offline     17179549184 0:1.0      noencl <sd6a>
```

Chunk *sd1a* shows up as *Offline*. This is a mirror so my data is still available, but I need to replace that drive before the remaining disk fails.

Repairing Volumes

First, find something to replace the failed disk. It must be at least as large as the smallest drive in the array. Drive *sd6* failed, but drive *sd7* is already installed as a warm standby. Use the −R flag to bioctl to specify a chunk to replace the failed chunk.

```
# bioctl -R /dev/sd7a sd10
softraid0: rebuild of sd10 started on sd7a
```

If you check the softraid status, you'll see something like this.

```
# bioctl sd5
Volume        Status              Size Device
softraid0 0 Rebuild     17179549184 sd10       RAID1 2% done
          0 Online      17179549184 0:0.0      noencl <sd5a>
          1 Rebuild     17179549184 0:1.0      noencl <sd7a>
```

The entry for *sd5* is in a *Rebuild* state. It is 2% complete. Similarly, drive 1 is in *Rebuild* state. You might as well walk away, this is going to take a while. A rebuild traverses the entire disk, including all blank space.

Multiple Softraid Volumes

You can have multiple softraid volumes on one host. Many organizations require mirrored boot drives, but want their databases on RAID-5. OpenBSD does this just fine.

```
# bioctl softraid0
Volume         Status              Size Device
softraid0 0 Online       17179549184 sd10       RAID1
          0 Online       17179549184 0:0.0       noencl <sd5a>
          1 Online       17179549184 0:1.0       noencl <sd7a>
softraid0 1 Online       34359083008 sd11       RAID5
          0 Online       17179549184 1:0.0       noencl <sd6a>
          1 Online       17179549184 1:1.0       noencl <sd8a>
          2 Online       17179549184 1:2.0       noencl <sd9a>
```

The first entry has been assigned device node *sd5* and uses RAID1. It has two chunks, *sd5a* and *sd7a*.

The second entry, *sd11*, uses RAID5. It uses chunks *sd6a*, *sd8a*, and *sd9a*.

Note that both of these are tied to device *softraid0*. This device node represents the softraid interface, not a specific softraid volume. You won't ever see a */dev/softraid1*.

Detaching a Volume

Use the -d flag to detach a volume. You must use the volume's device node. Here I remove the RAID5 volume from the previous section.

```
# bioctl -d sd6
```

There's no confirmation dialog. OpenBSD assumes you know what you're doing.

Reattaching a Volume

The manual says that -c creates a volume, but that's slightly misleading. You use -c to initialize a brand new volume, yes. You also use it to attach an existing-but-not-active softraid. Reattach a detached volume with the exact same `bioctl` command you used to initialize it.

Whenever you use -c, bioctl checks the specified chunks for metadata. If it sees no softraid metadata on any of the chunks, it initializes a new softraid. If it sees metadata that match the discipline you declare, it activates those disks and creates the softraid virtual volume. If bioctl finds softraid metadata for a different discipline, it errors out. If you want to reuse those chunks in a different sort of softraid, you must destroy the volume.

Destroying a Softraid

Suppose I detach my RAID-5 volume and want to reuse those chunks in a three-way mirror.

```
# bioctl -c 1 -l sd2a,sd3a,sd4a softraid0
softraid0: volume level does not match metadata level
```

Each partition used as a chunk has a few bytes of softraid metadata at the beginning. Softraid sees this metadata and refuses to overwrite it. To reuse a disk, overwrite this metadata and relabel the disk.

```
# dd if=/dev/zero bs=1m count=1 of=/dev/sd2a
# dd if=/dev/zero bs=1m count=1 of=/dev/sd3a
# dd if=/dev/zero bs=1m count=1 of=/dev/sd4a
```

I can now partition and reuse these disks in a different type of softraid.

Softraid and /etc/fstab

OpenBSD reattaches all existing softraids automatically at boot. Device nodes are especially untrustworthy with RAID, so be absolutely certain you use DUIDs in */etc/fstab*.

```
3dc58c1f07ab5bf8.d /var/mysql ffs rw,nodev,noexec,nosuid,noauto 0 0
```

Despite what you will read in years and years of mailing list posts and blog articles, automatic configuration of softraid at boot basically just works.

Installing to a Mirror

On popular hardware like amd64 and arm64 you can boot off a mirrored softraid volume. The installer doesn't have general support for such installations, however, so you must manually set up the softraid before installing. The next chapter uses a similar process for encrypted installs.

Boot your install media, and drop into the shell. Set up your softraid before anything else.[20]

```
Welcome to the OpenBSD/amd64 7.2 installation program.
(I)nstall, (U)pgrade, (A)utoinstall or (S)hell? s
#
```

We're now working inside a super-tiny OpenBSD install, containing the bare minimum tools needed to get the operating system on a disk. Many commands are unavailable. The root partition is a memory disk with a few bytes free, but the memory disk is so snug that the installer doesn't create device nodes until they're needed. If necessary you can write a couple tiny scratch files in /tmp, but be parsimonious.

Start by asking OpenBSD what disks it thinks it has installed.

```
# sysctl hw.disknames
hw.disknames=cd0:,sd0:,sd1:,sd2:,sd3:,
  sd4:,rd0:5363551877f10557
```

The memory disk *rd0* is read from the installation CD in *cd0*. Other than those, we have disks *sd0* through *sd4*. I put five disks on this SAS controller, so that's what I would expect. I want to install the boot mirror on disks *sd0* and *sd1*. First, we need device nodes.

```
# cd /dev
# sh MAKEDEV sd0 sd1
```

---

[20]   Always do the hard part first. Front-load failure.

Any extra junk at the front of the disk might confuse the installer. Blow away any existing partition tables, disklabels, or other metadata at the front of each disk. I'm writing 10MB here, to create enough blank space to cover not just the front of the disk but also the softraid metadata and anything else that might possibly be in there.

```
# dd if=/dev/zero bs=1m count=10 of=/dev/sd0c
# dd if=/dev/zero bs=1m count=10 of=/dev/sd1c
```

The disks need partitions. Set both to GPT, entirely dedicated to OpenBSD. (You can use MBR on older hardware or EFI-free virtual systems.)

```
# fdisk -gy -b960 sd0
Writing GPT.
# fdisk -gy -b960 sd1
Writing GPT.
```

Now label both disks with a single OpenBSD partition of type *raid*.

```
# disklabel -E sd0
Label editor (enter '?' for help at any prompt)
sd0> a
partition: [a]
offset: [64]
size: [33554335]
FS type: [4.2BSD] raid
sd0*> w
sd0> q
```

Repeat the process for disk *sd1*.

The disks are ready for softraid. Create the mirror.

```
# bioctl -c 1 -l /dev/sd0a,/dev/sd1a softraid0
sd5 at scsibus2 targ 1 lun 0: <OPENBSD, SR RAID 1, 006>
sd5: 16383MB, 512 bytes/sector, 33553807 sectors
softraid0: RAID 1 volume attached as sd5
```

Our mirror is identified as disk *sd5*. Make a device node for it.

```
# sh MAKEDEV sd5
```

Exiting the shell will return you to the installer prompt. This time, begin installing. Once you set up the network and create an unprivileged account, you get to choose the disk. Pick your softraid device.

```
Available disks are: sd0 sd1 sd2 sd3 sd4 sd5.
Which disk is the root disk? ('?' for details) [sd0] sd5
```

Do the rest of the install normally. Reboot, and you'll come up in your new mirrored install.

Software-driven RAID is cool, but you know what's a pretty neat idea? *Encrypted* data storage.

"On this utterly insignificant blue-green planet, the ape-descended sysadmins are so amazingly primitive that they still think encrypted data storage is a pretty neat idea."

—Hitchhiker's Guide to OpenBSD

Chapter 8: Encrypted Storage

Hard drives are vulnerable to data theft, by virtue of being physical things that can be stolen. If someone takes your laptop, they take your data. A server pillaged from a remote data center will surrender all your secrets. What's in memory evaporates when the thief pulls the power cord, but what's on disk is forever.

Before leaping straight to "I must encrypt everything," however, consider your risks. I have seen more data loss due to unnecessarily encrypted disks than I have data protected by being encrypted at rest. I've hung around with sysadmins for decades, and most of us exist at the limits of tolerable complexity. We keep discovering new tricks and using them to make our systems more and more complicated until we overload and bulldoze it all. Disk encryption is another complexity. If someone steals the bag containing your OpenBSD laptop, are they targeting your data or your resaleable hardware? Chances are that they'll take one look at the login screen and either fling the thing in the nearest bin or take it to a buddy who can install Windows on it. If your laptop is stolen, you revoke its SSH key on all your servers and carry on.[21]

Some folks sincerely need to encrypt data at rest, though. They handle personally identifiable data, such as medical records. Or maybe they're relief workers in war zones and a laptop will be stolen specifically so names of targets can be taken from the hard drive. On

---

[21]   I won't insult you by asking if every workstation has its own unique SSH authentication keys. OpenBSD users are among the elite who wouldn't dream of doing anything so sloppy as reusing keys.

rare occasions, disk encryption is a convenience. If the regulations governing your organization say that disks must be scrambled before being discarded, encrypting them at install time handles that for you. Destroy the keys and the disks are useless.

OpenBSD's disk encryption is generally considered computationally unbreakable. If your data is sufficiently valuable, that's great for the data and bad for you. Where practical computational cryptanalysis ends, rubber hose cryptanalysis begins.

If you want to encrypt your disks because you want to learn how to manage encrypted disks, or because you work with snoops, that's valid. Keep good backups of any important data, allocate time and energy to managing the complexity, and pay attention.

Many sysadmins have very strong opinions on disk encryption, and consider opposing arguments a load of blowfish kidneys. The best way to have peace is to make the best decision you can based on available information and not tell anyone what you picked.

Encrypted Storage Prerequisites

OpenBSD implements storage encryption as a softraid discipline. It encrypts partitions, called *chunks*, creating encrypted volumes. Yes, you can create a single partition that covers the entire disk, but the distinction is important for managing the volume.

The *crypto* discipline encrypts single chunks in AES in XTS mode. The softraid discipline 1C encrypts mirrors. You cannot encrypt RAID-5 volumes at the filesystem level.

If any of this confused you, review Chapter 7 before proceeding.

If OpenBSD only encrypts chunks, what about full disk encryption? *Full disk encryption*, or *FDE*, is marketing fluff. No disk on any popular computing platform is truly, 100%, LBA-0-to-the-end encrypted. If nothing else, the hardware must be able to find and decipher the partition table and the boot loader. Vendors call it FDE because nobody would be interested in "nearly-all-of-the-disk encryption." A properly configured encrypted softraid is as much "full disk encryption" as any other vendor's FDE.

Disk Randomization

Most storage devices ship fully loaded with zeroes, except for SSDs that arrive full of ones. Encrypting a filesystem on them stands out like specks of paint on a white wall. The presence of data tells the attacker which parts of the disk to focus on. Cover your chunks with randomness before creating the partition. This takes a while, but it's a one-time process. Here I randomize the contents of volume *sd3*.

```
# dd if=/dev/urandom of=/dev/sd3c bs=1m
```

If the mirror's chunks have different background randomness, a sufficiently dedicated attacker could compare the two disk images and pick out the parts where the two disks are identical. Those are the filesystem. The attacker can ignore the rest.

To avoid this, randomize your volume after creating it but before writing the disklabel or creating the filesystem.

Passphrases and Keydisks

Decrypting the volume requires a key. This could be a passphrase, or a separate storage device called a *keydisk*. The key must be provided when attaching the volume.

Passphrases must be typed in to attach the volume. If OpenBSD is installed on an encrypted volume, you have to type the passphrase at boot. They make sense for laptops, or servers where you have reliable console access. Exactly like passphrases for any other sort of encryption, disk encryption passphrases should be at least a few words long and contain a bunch of different characters. Anyone who has the passphrase can decrypt the volume. Note that the passphrase is not the encryption key. The passphrase is used to encrypt the on-disk encryption key. This lets you change the passphrase without rewriting the entire volume.

The most common keydisk is a small flash drive. It must be plugged into the machine at boot time. If you're using disk encryption to pre-emptively scramble drives so you can easily dispose of them, a keydisk is reasonable. You might also use a keydisk for regulatory requirements, or to satisfy separation of privilege rules.

Which should you use? That depends on your threat model and situation. If I want to encrypt storage on my host `towel`, choosing the best key method demands knowing exactly where `towel` is. The best method for a datacenter might differ from a local server or your laptop. Choose the one that will meet your needs with the least amount of pain.

Keydisk Management

An on-disk key is only one megabyte, so you can use any storage media down to and including a 1.544MB floppy disk. I'll prepare keydisks from inexpensive flash drives. Flash drives—especially inexpensive ones—support a limited number of writes, so I won't use the remaining space on the disk for anything.

The flash drive shows up as */dev/sd4* on this system. First, give it a partition table and then create a 1MB disklabel partition.

```
# fdisk -gy sd4
# disklabel -E sd4
Label editor (enter '?' for help at any prompt)
sd4> a
partition: [a] p
offset: [64]
size: [4162463] 1m
FS type: [4.2BSD] raid
sd4*> w
sd4> q
No label changes.
```

This is slightly different than our usual disklabel. I use partition *p* for my key, because while most disks have partition *a* very few have a *p*. If I plug in a OpenBSD install drive instead of the flash drive, I want the decryption attempt to fail before the system even tries to decrypt anything. The size is only 1 megabyte, and the filesystem type is RAID. Write the label and exit disklabel(8).

When you use bioctl(8) to create the encrypted device, use the -k flag to specify the keydisk device. It will generate a key, write it to the keydisk, and use that key to encrypt the volume. Immediately copy the key disk to an image file. Include the host name in the image file, so you can use it later.

```
# dd if=/dev/sd4p bs=8192 skip=1 of=keydisk-towel.img
```

That keydisk image is vital to the encrypted volume. Immediately copy it to a different, secure host. Partition your second flash drive in the same way as the main key, and restore the backed-up key onto that key. Don't lose your encrypted volume because a cheap flash drive failed—with a backup key, losing the volume requires the failure of *two* cheap flash drives. Here I copy the key onto /dev/sd5p.

```
# dd if=keydisk-towel.img bs=8192 seek=1 of=/dev/sd5p
```

Once you verify that the duplicate key works, you can deploy your keydisk-encrypted volume.

Encryption Disciplines

OpenBSD supports two disciplines for encrypted softraids, CRYPTO and RAID-1C.

The CRYPTO discipline encrypts a single chunk. It has no redundancy. Use it for single-drive systems and removable media. The capital C flag to bioctl(8) sets the CRYPTO discipline.

The RAID-1C discipline encrypts a mirror. Use this for hosts with multiple drives. The bioctl flag 1C sets RAID-1C.

Creating Encrypted Volumes

I want to use disk sd3 as an encrypted volume on an existing OpenBSD install. This might be an internal or external disk, it doesn't matter. First, create an OpenBSD partition that covers the entire disk. It must use a filesystem type of *RAID*, exactly like any other softraid device.

```
# disklabel -E sd3
sd3> a a
offset: [64]
size: [1953525071]
FS type: [4.2BSD] raid
sd3*> w
sd3> q
```

This partition is now ready to become a softraid volume. The only difference between the command to create an encrypted volume and any other kind of volume is the discipline. The -c option to bioctl lets you set the discipline. Indicate the *crypto* discipline with a C. Set the device with -l.

```
# bioctl -c C -l sd3a softraid0
New passphrase:
Re-type passphrase:
softraid0: CRYPTO volume attached as sd5
```

I did not specify a keydisk, so I am prompted for a passphrase. I must enter the passphrase any time I attach the volume.

If I want my encrypted volume to use a keydisk, I must specify the keydisk device with -k. Here I make partition *sd2a* the chunk for an encrypted volume, using keydisk *sd4p*.

```
# bioctl -c C -k sd4p -l sd2a softraid0
softraid0: CRYPTO volume attached as sd5
```

In either case, the new volume is blank.

It's possible for the existing random data on the underlying partitions to confuse tools like fdisk(8) and disklabel(8). Blank out the first megabyte of the new devices before creating partitions.

```
# dd if=/dev/zero bs=1m count=1 of=/dev/sd5c
# fdisk -gy sd5
# disklabel -E sd5
```

Once the device has a disklabel partition, I can put a filesystem on it.

```
# newfs /dev/rsd5a
```

I must use `fdisk` and `disklabel` to create partitions on it, then run `newfs` to give it a filesystem.

Managing Encrypted Volumes

Managing encrypted volumes isn't very different from managing unencrypted ones, except that if you do it wrong your data evaporates in a puff of logic.

Attach, Detach, and Destroy

Just as with an unencrypted softraid, use the -c option to `bioctl` to attach an existing encrypted volume. You'll be prompted for the passphrase.

```
# bioctl -c 1C -l sd2a,sd3a softraid0
Passphrase:
```

If the command is correct, softraid will attach the volume. If no metadata exists `bioctl` will create a new softraid, but if the existing metadata is incorrect the command gives an error.

Detach an encrypted softraid exactly as you would an unencrypted one.

```
# bioctl -d sd5
```

If you want to reuse the chunks in a different softraid, you must overwrite the softraid metadata at the front of the chunk.

```
# dd if=/dev/zero bs=1m count=1 of=/dev/sd2a
# dd if=/dev/zero bs=1m count=1 of=/dev/sd3a
```

Changing Passphrases

When you have reason to believe that your passphrase is no longer secure, such as if a team member gets picked up by an alien spacecraft or something, change it with the -P option to `bioctl`.

```
# bioctl -P sd5
Old passphrase:
New passphrase:
Re-type passphrase:
```

Much as with SSH passphrases, a softraid passphrase is not the volume's encryption key. Usable passphrases make really terrible encryption keys. Rather, the passphrase is used to encrypt the encryption key. You can thus change the passphrase without rewriting the entire volume.

Passphrases on the Command Line

Giving the passphrase on the command line is a terrible idea. It shows up in the system process list. You'll probably put it in plain text in a script somewhere as well. Your threat model might permit poorly managing encrypted disks, though, so here's how you do it.

The -s option to bioctl(8) tells it to read the passphrase from standard input rather than a prompt. This lets you feed the passphrase in via a pipe.

```
# echo 'Lucas is an idiot' | \
  bioctl -c 1C -l sd2a,sd3a -s softraid0
softraid0: RAID 1C volume attached as sd5
```

You don't have to use echo. If you want to write a complicated script that fetches the passphrase from a remote database, that's fine too. Whatever horrible solution you come up with is fine.

Passphrases in a File

Storing your passphrase in a file is slightly less bad than reading the passphrase from standard input. The file must be owned by root:wheel and have a mode of 600. Use the -p option to tell bioctl to read the file.

```
# bioctl -c 1C -l sd2a,sd3a \
  -p /root/mirror1passphrase softraid0
```

Should you stash the passphrase in a file? That depends wholly on the threats to your data.

Encrypted Volumes at Boot

OpenBSD automatically attaches encrypted volumes with a keydisk at boot, if the keydisk is plugged in. If you configure full disk encryption for your boot disk, as per Chapter 9, you'll be prompted for the passphrase at boot. A system with a mix of encrypted and unencrypted filesystems needs special handling at boot, however.

If you use a passphrase, you must either reattach the device by hand or use an */etc/rc.local* script. The catch is, disk devices might renumber during a reboot. If you want to reliably attach encrypted volumes at boot, your script must use DUIDs. At the command line, you would do something nice and friendly like this.

```
# bioctl -c 1C -l sd2a,sd3a -k sd4p softraid0
```

In */etc/rc.local*, that becomes this.

```
bioctl -c 1C -l 1e44b881a9544d5d.a,10c1c02e37d44886.a \
   -p /root/passphrase softraid0
mount /var/mysql
```

Fortunately you won't have to type this out.

You'll also want an */etc/fstab* entry to mount this volume. Be sure to use the DUID there as well, and mark it `noauto`. Add a mount(8) command to *rc.local* to automatically mount the filesystem. You might need to add other commands as well. This particular encrypted softraid is for */var/mysql*, so I can't start `mysqld` until after the softraid mounts.

At system shutdown, OpenBSD automatically unmounts and detaches all softraid volumes.

Installing to an Encrypted Volume

Let's pull everything together and install OpenBSD on an encrypted volume. As of OpenBSD 7.2, you can only boot from an encrypted mirror on amd64 and Sparc64 hardware. Fortunately, amd64 is the most common hardware these days. Boot the installer and break into the shell.

```
Welcome to the OpenBSD/amd64 7.2 installation program.
(I)nstall, (U)pgrade, (A)utoinstall or (S)hell? s
```

First, let's find out which disks OpenBSD found.

```
# sysctl hw.disknames
hw.disknames=sd0:,sd1:,cd0:,rd0:6d570a5ceaa294c7
```

Disks *sd0* and *sd1* are SAS disks. I'm booting off a CD, so it shows up as *cd0*. Finally, the *rd* recovery disk image is the OpenBSD install environment. If anything extra had shown up, I'd have to figure out what it was and where it came from. We need a device node for every disk, and one extra for the encrypted volume.

```
# cd /dev
# sh MAKEDEV sd0 sd1 sd2
```

Once this finishes, partition the disk. This is the twenty-first century, so use GPT.

```
# fdisk -gy -b 960 sd0
Writing GPT.
# fdisk -gy -b 960 sd1
Writing GPT.
```

Both disks are identical, so give them a single disklabel partition covering all the free space. Make it of type RAID, so softraid will accept it.

```
# disklabel -E sd0
Label editor (enter '?' for help at any prompt)
sd0> a a
offset: [1024]
size: [33553375]
FS type: [4.2BSD] raid
sd0*> w
sd0> q
```

Do the same for disk *sd1*.

Now I can assemble the mirror. My bureaucratic, officious manager wants this machine to be bootable only with a passphrase, so I make a note to be unavailable the first time it crashes and someone must drive to the datacenter. Here I create an encrypted mirror protected with a passphrase.

```
# bioctl -c 1C -l sd0a,sd1a softraid0
New passphrase:
Re-type passphrase:
sd2 at scsibus1 targ 1 lun 0: <OPENBSD, SR RAID 1C, 006>
sd2: 16383MB, 512 bytes/sector, 33552847 sectors
softraid0: RAID 1C volume attached as sd2
```

To be sure that someone can drive to the datacenter and boot the machine in the unlikely event of my absence, I write down the passphrase and give it to my manager.

Our new volume is *sd2*. Fill it with randomness.

```
# dd if=/dev/urandom of=/dev/sd2c bs=1m
```

This will take a while. Go get some tea.

To avoid confusing the kernel when it goes looking for a boot loader or filesystem table, zero out the volume's first megabyte.

```
# dd if=/dev/zero bs=1m count=1 of=/dev/rsd2c
```

We are now ready to install OpenBSD. Exit the shell and begin the install.

```
# exit
erase ^?, werase ^W, kill ^U, intr ^C, status ^T

Welcome to the OpenBSD/amd64 7.2 installation program.
(I)nstall, (U)pgrade, (A)utoinstall or (S)hell? i
…
```

Proceed as normal, until you are asked to choose a disk. Be sure to enter your encrypted volume, and use a GPT partition table on it.

```
Available disks are: sd0 sd1 sd2.
Which disk is the root disk? ('?' for details) [sd0] sd2
…
```

Once the install finishes, reboot. The early stage of the boot should show something like this.

```
probing: pc0 com0 mem[640K 989M 348K 16M 4M]
disk: hd0 hd1 cd0 sr0*
>> OpenBSD/amd64 BOOTX64 3.62
Passphrase:
```

Enter your passphrase. You'll be rewarded with a boot prompt.

```
>> OpenBSD/amd64 BOOTX64 3.62
boot>
```

Ignore it, and in a few seconds the timeout will lapse and the system will boot.

Congratulations! You now have a mirrored encrypted boot drive.

With this and the rest of this book, you have as good a grip on OpenBSD storage as anyone who isn't an OpenBSD developer. You can design and install your storage to work exactly the way you want. Any remaining system administration tasks, like users and software and debugging, are left as an exercise for the reader.

"Oracle code is of course the third worst in the Universe. The very worst code of all is by M W Lucas of Detroit, Michigan, Earth."

—Hitchhikers Guide to OpenBSD

Afterword

Filesystems. Loathe them or ignore them, you can't like them. Disk management is the core task of system administration, and OpenBSD disk management demands more thought than most. Configuring your disks correctly makes everything else easier. Configuring disks poorly means struggling until you reinstall. OpenBSD's storage stack has been continually debugged for decades. It might not have fancy features, but it is incredibly reliable.

This is my tenth book that's basically about filesystems. Sometimes filesystems plus special sauce, sure, but basically it's all filesystems all the time around this joint. I'm not saying that pure desperation to find something even modestly amusing about the topic drove me to use Douglas Adams' work as a motif, but I was purely desperate to find anything about the topic even modestly amusing. If you ever find yourself in a similar situation and attempt the same solution, do establish your Standard Reference Hitchhikers' Guide before sending your work to review. If you use the 1981 BBC TV show when your copyeditor has memorized the books, hilarity will *not* ensue.

If OpenBSD's storage stack doesn't include something you want, the developers await your patches with interest. All I can say is: *we apologize for the inconvenience.*

Sponsors

These grand folks contributed to keep me alive as I worked on this book. Naming them in the book is a poor reward for such generosity, but it's the reward I promised, so here it is. If you'd like to be notified the next time a sponsorship is available so you can add your name to the list, sign up for my sponsors mailing list at https://mwl.io.

Lucas Raab
Russell Folk
William Allaire
tanamar corporation
Chris Dunbar
Bob Eager
Niall Navin
Rogier Krieger
David Hansen
Patrick Bucher
Marcus Neuendorf
Cal Ledsham
Gordon Carrie
Alexander Shendi
Bernd Kohler
Manuel Solis Aguero
Eric LeBlanc
Paul Covello

Stefan Johnson
Brad Sliger
Florian Viehweger
Reinis Martinsons
Lutz Weber
Nathan Madsen
Lucas Raab
Paul Gatling
Craig Maloney
Phi Network Systems
Franz Bettag
Daniel Parriott
Anthony Issa
Russell Folk
Callan Ledsham
HamBSD
Eric LeBlanc

About the Author

More Tech Books from Michael W Lucas

Absolute BSD
Absolute OpenBSD (1st and 2nd edition)
Cisco Routers for the Desperate (1st and 2nd edition)
PGP and GPG
Absolute FreeBSD (2nd and 3rd edition)
Network Flow Analysis

the IT Mastery Series

SSH Mastery (1st and 2nd edition)
DNSSEC Mastery (1st and 2nd edition)
Sudo Mastery (1st and 2nd edition)
FreeBSD Mastery: Storage Essentials
Networking for Systems Administrators
Tarsnap Mastery
FreeBSD Mastery: ZFS
FreeBSD Mastery: Specialty Filesystems
FreeBSD Mastery: Advanced ZFS
PAM Mastery
Relayd and Httpd Mastery
Ed Mastery
FreeBSD Mastery: Jails
SNMP Mastery
TLS Mastery

The Networknomicon

Other Nonfiction

Domesticate Your Badgers
Cash Flow For Creators
Only Footnotes

Novels and Collections (as Michael Warren Lucas)

Immortal Clay – Kipuka Blues – Butterfly Stomp Waltz – Terrapin Sky Tango
Forever Falls – Hydrogen Sleets – Drinking Heavy Water
Aidan Redding Against the Universes – $ git commit murder – $ git sync murder
Prohibition Orcs – Frozen Talons – Vicious Redemption – Devotion and Corrosion

See your local bookstore for more!

Index

www.ingramcontent.com/pod-product-compliance
Lightning Source LLC
Chambersburg PA
CBHW041637050326

40690CB00026B/5253